YOU COULDN'T HAVE TOLD ME BEFORE I STARTED MY BUSINESS

Jeff Roziere & Cathy Snelgrove

117 10th Street
Brandon, Manitoba
R7A 4E7

www.siere.ca

ABOUT THE AUTHORS

Jeff and Cathy spent the early part of their careers in executive management positions in both the private and public sectors, working for organizations such as Boeing Canada, City of Brandon, Behlen Industries and more.

After starting Siere Solutions, they worked with and challenged numerous small- to medium-sized business leaders and owners to create outstanding business results in their companies. Their diverse experience in operations, sales, human resources, Lean, and safety systems allows them to bring a unique perspective to the ins and outs of running a business in changing times. Combining the knowledge of human psychology with what it takes to generate peak performance, they leave their clients always asking for more.

At Siere, we work with you to maximize the profitability of your business – guaranteed. Visit our website; www.siere.ca to learn more.

Or send us your comments, feedback or success stories to office@siere.ca. We would love to hear from you. You never know, we may showcase those stories in one of our upcoming books, or on our various pages.

Table of Contents

INTRODUCTION

We know you picked this book up for of one of two reasons. Either A, you have recently started your own business and are wondering if you made the right decision; or B, you are thinking about starting your own business, and want to make sure you are making the right decision.

It seems today, everybody is thinking about starting up their own business and we find this to be really exciting. We believe operating your own business can be one of the most amazing challenges you will ever take on. Certainly there a lot of things to consider in choosing this path, however we will tell you first hand, you will never gain the type of experience you will get from operating your own business, doing anything else.

I remember when I was working for the Boeing Company, sitting beside a gentleman on an airplane to Seattle. Somewhere in the two hour flight, we struck up a conversation and before long I learned he owned a hot air balloon company. His company flew balloons; however what intrigued me even more was they also made them. They were the company that made all the custom balloons you would see in Canada, representing all kinds of companies. I was fascinated by his story; how he had started out in his garage and how the company had grown over the years. I remember thinking to myself, what a great journey he has had and how wonderful it would be to be a part of something like that. How inspiring to know you had created something from the ground up and to know you were making a difference in the world.

As the conversation turned to me and what I did, I told him I worked for the Boeing Company, in management, in one of the manufacturing plants. He asked a lot of questions about what specifically I did and what it was like to work for such an amazing company. We shared some funny antidotal stories and after a time, fell silent. It was as the captain came on and told us we needed to get our things together for landing I turned to the gentleman and said to him, one day I really hoped to own my own company. He didn't say anything for a moment, and then finally said, "If there is one piece of advice I can give you, don't go into business for yourself." I was stunned. In a million years I would never have anticipated he would say such a thing! After all, look how incredible his story was. When I asked him why he replied, "It is hard work running your own company. You never have any time because you have to work like a dog; in order to keep everything going. If I had it to do all over there is no way I would do it again! You have a great job which pays you really well I assume and you will have a happier life, if you stay doing what you are doing, trust me."

This story stayed in my head for a long time because I remember how it didn't seem to make sense to me at the time. I had always wanted to start my own business, and remember even coming out of college and university believing my job was just going to be a brief stopover. I knew one day I would own my own company. Sure, I could have understood the advice if he hadn't been successful, however by all accounts he seemed to have done very well. That said, what would have him give this sort of advice to me? This same story played over and over, even as the two of us were discussing the possibility of starting our own business. It had me question whether we were doing the right thing and if it could be we were making a huge mistake. We both had incredible executive management positions which paid well and had lots of benefits. Was it really smart of us to choose to throw all of this away, in pursuit of something which certainly wasn't guaranteed?

Have you ever noticed for every significant lifetime event, there are always people who are more than willing to give you advice? Remember when you were young and in school, when sure enough the dreaded question would come up, "So, what are you going to do, when you graduate?" You now must realize in some cases, this was really a rhetorical question. They were only asking you the question so they could tell you what they thought you should do. They would give you their ideas, and tell you about the things they wish they had or hadn't done. It wasn't that they didn't care about you and your ideas. In some cases it was probably more like they cared for you too much. They needed to share with you their wisdom so you wouldn't make the same mistakes and have the regrets they did. They were really trying to be helpful.

In some cases you may have listened to them and in others you probably totally disregarded what they had to say. Each of us is surrounded by a world of advice and some of it can be useful. However often times, the people who are giving the advice have never in fact done what you are looking to do. Just listen to the people around you who have an opinion about things which they know little, if anything, about. It will be the parent who tells the teacher how to teach. It will be the father-in-law who tells you how to fix something. So often advice comes from the person who has never done it. It will be the person who has never run a business, who will tell you what you need to do. It is human nature to want to give advice. I remember buying a home with a pool and how many people told me how much work they were. After a decade in the home, as I was selling it I remember some prospective buyers asking and commenting on the work of a pool. It really wasn't a lot of work in comparison to any other yard work and I know those people with pools share my thoughts. It is funny how many times those who don't have any experience to base on something, claim to know.

We laugh about it now, but when the two of us decided to get into business together there were people who asked each one of us about whether we thought we were making the best decision in partnering with the other. This happened to both of us. The funny thing is we shared few common friends who really knew both of us at the point we decided to get into business. For the most part, they only knew of us by name and by the position we held at the time. When they asked those questions, we would wonder what their concern was really about. Of course, they couldn't understand our thinking, no matter how much we tried to explain. They had never seen us work together and how much respect we have for each other. They didn't know what strengths each of us brought to the table and for some of them they didn't even know what it was we were going to be doing. We wondered how it was they seemed to be so concerned.

At the time we didn't understand what we know now and believed. They were literally talking about the potential faults of the other person. As a result, we would spend those moments trying to justify our position and telling them all the wonderful aspects of the partner we were getting into business with. In some cases, it would seem to squelch their worry, however in other cases, we would get, "Well, I hope you know what you are doing so you don't regret this decision later on." You know that one, as we are sure you might have heard it a time or two, yourself.

As we have continued to explore how the mind works in creating human performance in business, we know their words of advice, "let's be clear" were not for us! They were speaking their own fears from their own past experience. They were trying to understand how it was we could be so sure we were making the right decision, whether it was about the partnership, or more importantly about getting into business. They were testing us to make sure we had thought through all of the possible scenarios. It just had a surface appearance of advice giving, but we know

now they were really speaking their own fears.

We will tell you right up front, this book is going to appear to be about giving advice. However, in our case, we have been through all of these scenarios. We work with business in and around these aspects on a daily basis. Some of the things you read you may have even heard before, and we know in other cases you will notice we take a different spin on the world. For the purpose of this book; we would like you to look at the idea of advice in a different way. We know you will have already received a lot of advice. In some cases it will have been positive and in others, not so much. Advice can be easy to disregard when it doesn't fit what we want to hear and easy to accept, when it does. What we will ask you is rather than think of what we are saying as advice, think of it as us testing you. This might sound a little crazy at first however we know as you go out and create your business you are going to be tested, over and over again. At this point we think, you might as well understand how this works, now!

Our belief is anytime you decide you want to do something there will be forces around you which will test your conviction to do it. It really is meant to have you question whether what you are thinking or attempting to do is a good idea. Sure, you can disregard these tests or you can use them to your benefit. We know there are times when you choose to disregard something and yet it plays over and over in your mind. Every time you think about it, you question once again whether you are doing the right thing and over a period of time this will rack your confidence. If on the other hand, you choose to really listen to what is being said and choose to confront it in the moment, then you can resolve it once and for all. Think about these moments as your doubts playing out in front of you. You will now begin to notice the people around you speak your doubts and because they do sometimes, you may even get angry at them for doing so. You can choose to be angry or you can choose to build your conviction and have them disappear. It is a matter of listening to what is said and asking yourself the question, "Do I believe what they are saying?" If the answer is no, then let it go, and get focused on what you want. If the answer is yes, then ask yourself how it is you could be thinking this and then what is it you need to do right away to resolve it once and for all, for you.

For example, let's say you decided you want to run a marathon. As you tell people about what you want to do, you will hear people tell you about the "runner's wall" and about how hard the training is and about the fact you will have some joint pain, etc. Chances are you already know these things and will have had those same doubts play through your mind, when you were considering whether or not you wanted to take on this challenge. Once you made the decision and started the process of training, before long you noticed some of those things. However you evaluated them and decided you could handle them and you continued. You will have noticed the more conviction you had and the closer you got to your goal, by magic, this type of chatter in your environment suddenly seems to disappear. When it does, know unconsciously you have resolved those doubts for you. To do this, there were specific actions you took which had you resolve those doubts and as you did so, your conviction related to your goal increased. As your conviction to the goal increased, so did your environment in supporting you to achieve that specific goal. This is a natural law at work for you and it works both ways.

We believe in cause and effect and you have a choice about which side of the equation you sit on. You can be at effect to everything in your environment, including what you are thinking. Or you can be at cause for everything in your environment, again including what you are thinking. This is your choice. Cause is not about blaming yourself or others, it is a mind set. It is when you believe you have somehow, consciously or unconsciously created everything in your world as an avenue to learn and grow. Can we prove you have actually created everything? Of course not. However we do know, if you hold this thinking, you will also have the ability to create something different in the future. At the end of the day, when you are at effect to things you are powerless to change them - always. If you are blaming people and circumstance around you for the position you are in; you will have the need to "make" them change in order to release you from your cage. Even worse, they will become your excuse for not having what you want. We know at times you will spend a lot of time trying to get someone else to change. This is wasted energy because they don't change, only you can. If you put the same energy in to you, you will be further ahead. It is simply, about asking yourself, "How did I create this and for what purpose." If you can learn something from everything happening around you, you will continue to create new possibilities for you.

In reading this book, know we have been where you are. There have been moments when we questioned what we were doing and whether we were making the right choices. There have been challenges we created which have allowed us to thrive. There have been things we have been really successful at and there have been other ideas which didn't work out so well. Let us be honest with you, right now....you are going to make mistakes. The truth of the matter is we all do and it is the basis of learning and growing. As long as you take mistakes and view them as the means to learn and grow they are only feedback for you. There are some people who become paralyzed as soon as something goes wrong, and they spend much time hashing over the same old thing, in an attempt to somehow change the outcome. You cannot change the past. All you can do is move forward. What if what appeared to be a mistake, was really a step which in learning something prevented you from making an even bigger one? Have you ever thought of it that way? Things will happen, and just like a goalie in sports, if you only focus on the goal just scored on you, sure enough you won't see the next one coming at you. You need to stay focused on what you are creating and know if you do, the little things will resolve themselves.

We will tell you from our experience, there is no "one size fits all" solution. As an entrepreneur you need to continue to expand your flexibility which means you need to continually be pushing yourself. We call these our "ledge moments". Whether you have just started a business or are thinking about a business, you will know there is a ledge in front of you. There are lots of people who get to the ledge and choose to turn and run away from it, whereas there is another breed that faces them head on. Please know you have an incredible amount of potential within you, however it remains as potential until the moment you make the choice to actualize it. Potential is nothing until it is manifested into a result. Remember nothing is ever as good or as bad as you think it is in any given moment and the key is to recover quickly and to regain your focus.

We both love the work we do. We get to work with business leaders and entrepreneurs everyday to challenge them in their thinking and to ultimately drive incredible results for them and us. We are committed to seeing small to medium business grow, because as you know, they are the life breath of our economies. This book is intended to test you and to have you consider whether you are ready to take the leap. It is intended to provide you with a perspective which will strengthen your conviction about the path you are already on.

YOUR REASON FOR GETTING INTO BUSINESS

Resoundingly, when we ask individuals why it is they want to or why it is they decided to get into their own business, we hear two common themes. The first one is they want to be their own boss. They are tired of working for someone else and being told what to do and when to do it, which feeds into the second. I want to have control over my time. I want to be able to spend more time doing what it is I like to do and to spend more time with my family. In fact, if you had asked us when we got into business, we would have said exactly the same thing.

Here is the reality, and you can believe us or not. Nothing could be further from the truth. Running a business is not only a full time job...it is two full time jobs. One of the things we say is if you are going to get into a business you had better love what you are doing, because in fact you will live and breathe it, especially when you first get into business.

When you have a job and are working for someone else, you will certainly be busy doing the "technical" aspect of your job. There will be times when you are faced with meeting certain deadlines and other times when the amount of work may seem overwhelming, especially in today's business world. As companies have driven to be more efficient and competitive, without a doubt, there are more expectations and work load being placed on individuals. Depending on your work environment, there will be certain hours you need to put in and there will be specific times when you need to have completed your work. Chances are your vacation is coordinated with others in your organization and then is approved by your boss. We know this process can certainly be frustrating and can feel limiting to you at times. In some cases, individuals believe they are undercompensated or underappreciated in the organization.

Similarly, when you work in an organization, there can be times when decisions are made you might think hold no merit. There is the office politics and sometimes the structure of how things have to be done can seem to be crazy. You are clear if you were the one running the show you would do things entirely different. Even though you give your boss your thoughts and ideas, you might feel you are not being heard. In your present situation you may struggle with your boss and think he or she is focused on the wrong things, and perhaps even feel they make doing your job more difficult than it needs to be. You know you are full of lots of really great ideas, however at times may feel like your creativity and flexibility are being stifled. We are sure if you are thinking about starting your own business or have just got into your own business, some of this will apply to you, in even having considered stepping out. For these reasons, you will have looked at the other side and thought to yourself, maybe the "grass is greener over there".

In some aspects, the "grass is greener" on the other side however, please know it is because it has been painted green, not because it is different from the grass on your side. One of the first things you need to know is it doesn't matter who you talk to in business, they are going to tell you things are going well. Just for a moment think about it this way; if you were to walk into a store wanting to buy something and were told, "Things are so bad we are thinking about closing up shop." Would you buy from them? Just think about when the North American automobile industry was going through their challenges a couple of years ago, just prior to the government bail outs. How many people were lining up to buy their cars? Not many, and in fact this was part of the reason the foreign automobile companies did so well in those years. The only North American car company which did well was Ford because they were able to stand up and say they had positioned their company to not need the government assistance. How many times have you seen a business fold and in some cases, didn't even know it was going to happen. There can be facade in operating a business and of course you need to be seen as being successful. Business needs this simply to get people to come in the door. If you ask a business owner, "How is business?" of course they are going to tell you it is going well. In part, it is because you are there, standing right in front of them, so of course they want to sell to you and they need you to believe you have come to the right place. They will tell you what you need to hear in order to have you buy from them. We also chuckle when we hear business owners talk about being busy. Busy is a relative statement. Think about it, busy as compared to what? We always wonder if they are really busy, or if they are busy being busy. We don't know of an entrepreneur who would ever be too busy to capitalize on a new business venture. Do you think Donald Trump would say he was too busy? This leads us to our next point.

Now, let's talk about time. In a job, you are busy doing whatever it is you are hired to do. If you are writing reports, then that is what you are focused on, all day long. Sure there may be a lot of reports which need to be written however your focus is on writing reports. You certainly don't have to think about who is processing your pay cheque, who is coordinating your benefit package, who is making sure government taxes are being paid or who is ordering supplies. You don't have to worry about who is selling your services, who is developing the website and what it will look like, or who is sitting down with the bank to review your business and financial position. These are all being done behind the scenes, by other people in the organization. Now if you work for a small company, you may have a broader range of responsibilities. Still, rest assured there is someone else who is picking up the "stuff" you are not doing.

As soon as you become a business owner, guess what now falls to you to figure out? All of it! Sure you might decide you will hire a book keeper to do up your books however, you will still be the one who has to make sure there is the money in the bank to pay for the cheques written. You might hire someone else to develop your website, however, you will still be the one who is responsible for developing the content and making sure it is doing what it needs to do for your company as it is you who holds the vision. You might hire someone to do sales however, you will still be the one who has to hire and manage the person. So on top of the report writing you had before, you now also have new jobs and responsibilities to learn and perform. Part of the challenge is now you are in business and you are responsible for it all. It is not like you have the luxury of having three months to learn it, knowing that someone else will pick up the slack while you are doing so. You have to learn things on the fly and the learning curve for most is incredibly steep.

Anytime you take on a new job, you know it will take you a period of time to become proficient at what you are doing. A nice rule of thumb is it takes somewhere between three and six months, to come up the learning curve in a new job. As you get into business, you have probably already acknowledged getting your business off the ground is going to take an upfront commitment of time. You have told yourself you are prepared to do so, in order to ensure your success. It doesn't seem like a big deal because number one you are excited about what you are doing and number two, you will be making progress in achieving your dream. You are excited and more than prepared to put in the long hours. You will have warned your family up front you are going to need to spend some extra time building your business and they will be supportive, because after all it won't be forever, or so they think.

We will tell you the learning curve in business is nothing like the learning curve you go through in getting a new job. For one, generally speaking the work you do in a new job is repetitive, so after a while you get into a groove. You know what you need to do in order to be successful in the job and you learn all of the short cuts which make it easier. You do the processes over and over again until you become great at them. Where a business is different is, it is all about how well you can handle the variety of things you need to do. It is all about how you think about what you do, not in what you do. In some cases there will be those repetitive tasks, however there are other things you may not do again for months and then suddenly they will fall back on your plate. For example, you only file your corporate income taxes once a year, so each year it is like a whole new experience preparing the material for your accountant. The key is in how quickly you can reacquaint yourself with the task at hand and how fast you can move through it. The saying goes, "Time is Money" and it really is true when it comes to running a business.

In a job, regardless of the amount of time you spend on get something done, you are going to get the same pay cheque at the end of the week. If you have an "off" day, it is really no big deal when you spend a little longer on your coffee break. If you have a day when you are feeling under the weather, you can call in sick and depending on the size of company you work for and the type of work you do, you will probably still get paid. Absolutely if your performance is below standard you could find yourself out of a job, however for the most part, we will assume you have been successful. In a small business, every second you spend doing something which isn't generating you revenue is a second wasted. You can buy a lot of things in this world although you can never buy back time. You will know the times of day when you need to be focused on generating sales, so everything else will have a tendency to fall into the off times...thus the second job. You will find yourself, doing your paperwork and books during the evenings. You will find yourself at the office on Saturday and Sunday, just trying to catch up. You will find yourself thinking about your business day and night. You may even find yourself at a family function or event and if you are not looking at your watch anticipating what time it will end so you can get back to work, you will be rolling ideas around in your head about how to do things differently. Running a business is not a part time commitment. It needs to become a central focus in your life if you want to succeed beyond paying yourself a wage. Talk to any successful business owner and you will find the same perspective.

While we paint somewhat of a bleak picture in regards to time, we will tell you that you will become better at the understanding the important things and you will come to enjoy the variety and challenge. That is, if you don't already. Please understand, learning to run a business is certainly not a three to six month learning curve. It will take time and while you will be able to have a Friday afternoon off and you won't have to ask your boss for it, you will still likely have put in the time somewhere else. As you grow your business and add staff, of course it will be easier to get away although your time will then get portioned to include managing staff.

Now to the point of, "I will be my own boss and will get to decide what I want to do." Sure from moment to moment throughout the week, you will have more control over what you are doing. You will be the decision maker and there is good news and bad news about this. Sure you will have control of the business you are in. You will get to decide on the products and services you provide and you will have control over the clients and customers you will provide those offerings. However you will still have bosses!

The government will expect you are going to file your taxes and that you will pay your employees on time. Your insurance company will expect you are running your business in a way to minimize your risks. Regulators will expect you to meet certain regulatory requirements. The bankers will expect you are staying on side with them. Your clients and customers will demand a level of service and will have their own opinions about what you need and should be doing. Oh and don't forget about your employees. They will be the "you", you are today. They will have their own ideas about what needs to be done and when. They will want you to have the time to acknowledge the work they do and to demonstrate the value you see in them. They will expect you to have plans to grow the business, so they can succeed and grow with you. They will demand their issues be resolved right away so they can do their jobs. Your family will want to tell you that you are working too hard and you need to make time for the important things in life. If you think about it, you are simply trading one boss for many. We will tell you first hand, sometimes all these new bosses can be bigger pains than the one you may have right now. In leading an organization we know you will sincerely want everyone to be successful. You will want to help them and to listen to them. You will want to be a great coach and mentor however the challenge comes when you realize you are only one person.

As you get established, all of this becomes easier to balance. However for at least the first couple of years you need to be prepared for days when you recognize working for someone else was easier in a lot of ways. If you are looking to get into a business, make sure you are doing it for the right reasons. From our perspective, there is no way we would want to go back to working for someone else. In fact, we joke today about being unemployable. Running our businesses are one of the most rewarding things either of us has done; however just be aware you will work harder than you have ever have if you intend to succeed.

LOVE WHAT YOU DO

It may sound cliché, however it is the truth. In whatever business you choose to get into, you had best love what you do. As you are starting to understand, there will be times when things will get tough. From time to time your industry, your market, your competitors, your clients or customers and your employees will test your will to stay in the game. If you hate what you are doing, you will fail those tests and find yourself packing back to your old nine to five job. This will be the business owner with the series of failed attempts, who jumps from one business to the next, never completing the cycle and always reverting to the job. We think about it this way…if you hate what you do in your own business, then the work you do becomes a job.

We are sure you are asking, "So, what does loving what you do even mean and how would I know whether I do or don't?" Let's take the polar opposite of love. Let's talk about hate, recognizing that everything in between is "shades of grey". We believe too often people get into business with an idea which sits in a "shades of grey" category. That is they don't love it, nor do they hate it. For them, it is just kind of ok. It was something they thought they could make a go of. It was something they thought people would want or need and they would be willing to pay you for. For example, there are many house painters out there in the world. They deliver a service and people are willing to pay some amount of money for the service. Now, if you were to take a guess, how many house painters do you believe actually love what they do? Our guess is probably not very many, although they are running a business. How many business owners would you guess do not love what they are doing and therefore fall into doing "shades of grey work" which they could get paid for?

13

When you get into business, you are entering into an unconscious contract. It is the one that owns you...your time, your energy and your money. The only thing you own is how you feel about what you are doing. Love it or loathe it, it will be the thing you create and at a point through its growth, it will become an extension of you and who you are. Find something you love and choose to do it...be daft about it!

To be really successful in business, you need to be *daft*! That's right. You need to be daft, it is a requirement. So what does that mean? Let's look at the dictionary definition for a moment. Daft means to be;

1. senseless, stupid, or foolish.

2. insane; crazy.

3. *Scot.* merry; playful; frolicsome.[i]

Now think back and remember when you were a kid. There was something you were crazy about. It could have been a sport or a hobby, or simply some sort of past time. You loved what you were doing when you did it and you could have done it all the time. It was seemingly what you lived for and it became who you were at the time. You were insane, crazy, senseless and foolish when you were doing it and it made you feel alive and engaged. While you may have felt this, in the eyes of others you were all of those things and chances are you really didn't care what anyone else thought about what you were doing. You did what you did and you loved every moment of it and even more, couldn't get enough of it. This is the type of energy and enthusiasm you need to take with you into your business. Those people who have passion are the ones who are successful. We will tell you if you feel blah about your business, then those will be the kinds of results you will achieve. Find the thing you are crazy about and you will figure out how to be successful doing it.

So, you want to start or have started a business and are thinking, "What would it mean if you were to do something you loved, and we mean really loved." The people you are around....may see this and you as being silly. The nonsense you use to dream about was alright as a kid, but today you are an adult. You need to grow up, be smarter and do the right thing. They may even feel the need to save you from yourself.

As a kid when you loved your sport, you held the belief or maybe wanted to hold the belief you could do it forever. Think about the kids who, when asked, tell you they want to play for the NBA or the NHL. They are proud of their accomplishments and they feel good about what they are doing and they really do believe they could be this. However, over time the logical brain begins to take over. At this point you listened to the world tell you about the odds and perhaps you bought into the "only a few make it" belief. Prior to believing this, you did what you did and you were driving towards something. When you were on your game, you felt like a pro and in those moments you believed you could do anything.

We often say, "Someone has to make it, so why not you?" Wouldn't you agree? What if it was you who made it? We mean, why not. If someone is going to make it, does it need be someone else? We mean, if you really love it, why not you? From our perspective you have to be a little, or perhaps a whole lot "daft" in your love of your business idea to make it.

When we think of daft, we think of the following acronym;

*D*riven
*A*ttentive
*F*ocus
*T*hrifty

As a business owner you have to be **Driven**, burning the candle at both ends so to speak. As we have explained, chances are your nine to five days are over. You have to be driven to go get those new clients or customers and then deliver the product or service in answer to their needs. You need to be prepared to sell and market yourself 24/7 and to be proud of what you are creating. This is your new game. Oh and by the way, news flash…the friends and family who promise to buy your product or services as you planned your business are well meaning, but they will yield you very little…we will discuss this a little later on. You will have to be the one to sell you and your company. We will tell you first hand, you are the only one who can waive your banner. In this, you better be silly in love with what you are doing because the people you are selling to will know unconsciously. It has to burn within you, for you to have the energy needed to create and grow your business. You have to be driven.

We know most businesses are created based on what an entrepreneur sees around them. So for example, if the environment they are in is predominantly retail, then new entrepreneurs will lean towards creating more of that. If the environment is filled with construction companies, then guess what they will think they should get into? This is why we see pockets of expertise in various areas of our world. Think about Silicon Valley. It is the home of some of the largest technology companies, and there are thousands of small startup companies in this one region. How many startup technology companies do you see in your area? If you are getting into a business because you are seeing others around you doing it and yet, it does not excite you then it is the wrong company for you.

We understand it can be difficult to step out and do something different. However at the same time if you can provide something different and unique in your market, then you will also have a success different from everybody else. This takes drive because you will be challenging the norm. We know just the idea of starting or being in business for the first time may already be pushing you from your comfort zone so why not really push the envelope? You must strive to do new things and explore the world in the theme of your entrepreneurial spirit. How is it you would need to think about what you love to do, to do it in a way you can be compensated? How is it you would need to think about what you do, to have others want to use your product or service? We know when you are driven to do something and are really in love with the idea, you will find ways of getting it done that others will not and this is where the money is made. This is where you will do things others will think are not possible. Your drive will set you apart from the herd. Love what you do, and create a drive behind to do it. Create entrepreneurial drive.

The entrepreneur has to be **Attentive** to their world. As a business owner you will need to be attentive and hold consideration for many people and things in your business. Your clients or customers will always be central in your focus along with the products and services you offer. Your employees and finances need to have your attention. Your business environment, locally, nationally and maybe internationally will also need to have your attention. All of this requires you to open your focus to the entire world of your business. If your focus is only on the next day or the next customer or making the next dollar, you will miss the indicators that could either strengthen or harm your company. There have been many small and large companies who have failed because they were not able to see that a market was changing, or a technology was taking over an industry. If your focus is only "in" your business, we will tell you that you will find problems to keep you busy. There will always be something to do and it is easy to get caught up in the busy and to lose sight of a bigger picture. You have to work to expand your attention to the broader picture, to get to the point where you require less detail, albeit have increased ability to attend to the many things in your world.

Think about it this way. When you were a young kid or if you look at young kids in general, they have pretty short attention spans. When they want something, they want it now. Consequences play no part in it and they give up anything in the moment to have it, even if it potentially punishes them later on. Operating a business is about the long game. Of course there are things you will want to take advantage of right away, however at the same time you may want to wait out other things, for a bigger gain in the future. In order to be able to evaluate these options, you must be attentive to the bigger picture so you don't get caught in the here and now.

Keeping your eyes on many balls is to be attentive. You have to be aware of things here and now, and at the same time be thinking how other things may impact you in the future. Knowing you are moving your business forward on all fronts is to be attentive. When you love what you do, you will create attention in your business to all those things which matter. The life blood of your business is your customers or clients, your employees, your revenue, your expenses and your cash flow. All of these require attentiveness.

The entrepreneur requires **Focus** on where they are going and the ability to hold and sustain it over time. There will be many tests along the way and we know your ability to maintain focus on the outcome is important in creating your success. Those entrepreneurs who have a scattered focus on their outcome tend to jump down rabbit holes and end up in the abyss. They get lost without even realizing they have left the path. Get focused clearly on what you are creating and stay on the path.

We love to talk to business owners and challenge them to see how they hold their position of focus related to what they are doing and creating. We will check to see how focused and unwavering they are in their position? We will tell you most spin off easily and can get side tracked. For example, we talked to a business owner and she owned a house cleaning company. She had done really well over the years, however business had started to tail off and she told us she was thinking about getting into selling cleaning products. On the surface it might have seemed like a good idea, however she didn't have a store front location where people could come in and buy it so they were going to have to be delivered. On her existing clients she provided the cleaning products as part of her contract so there would be no ability to increase sales to them. This meant she was going to have to create an entirely different customer base. She was going to have to pay a different tax structure and hadn't even considered it, etc. As we talked to her, we started asking her about house cleaning and what she believed was going on in her market. Long story cut short, by the end of the conversation, she decided to offer spring and fall cleaning packages to augment her core business rather than offering cleaning products.

As a business owner you must get focused and hold the ability to remain focused on your goals, and outcomes. That is where you are taking your business. It's easy to find shiny bobbles, however those shiny bobbles can be off ramps away from your focus of what you want. Know in your focus, where you are going and what you are building in your business. Where is your industry going? What will your market look like eighteen months from now, five years from now, ten years from now? Will you be doing things differently? How can you capitalize on these things?

The entrepreneur requires the ability to be **Thrifty.** Please do not mix this up with being frugal or cheap. Thrifty is about being able to see and make a good deal and it also means knowing where to invest wisely in your business in order to have it grow. "Cash is King" in the game of business, so you need to constantly know how cash is moving in and out of your company. When you are attentive you are able to look at the bigger picture and know strategically where you can put money to work.

As we will discuss later, most new entrepreneurs have no idea how much cash it takes to launch and or run a business, and most really have no idea how to make cash flow work for them. They have a tendency to spend time, money and resources in areas of their business which have little impact to the bottom line. Being in business is about return on investment. If it doesn't add value, you don't need it or you shouldn't do it. Often business owners are afraid of leverage and borrowing, so they will pass up on amazing opportunities. Mostly they will tell themselves it is because they don't have the cash, but it generally comes to the fact they are lost when it comes to structuring deals. You need to invest in you and your company wisely if you intend to be in business. Learning what it means to be thrifty is where money is made.

Now, you understand what we mean when we say, "You need to be daft." In our fast paced world today, going into business and being responsible for your own success goes against the grain. This is a good thing. Just know when you decide to get into business, you need to take on the "succeed at all costs" thinking. You will show those around you how to succeed as you remain focused on what you are creating. You will experience one of the most rewarding and satisfying opportunities in operating your own business.

INVEST IN LEARNING

It was Albert Einstein who said, "Learning is not a product of schooling but the lifelong attempt to acquire it" and in the case of the entrepreneur, this is absolutely true. When we started our business we both had a lot of education and as a result, felt we were more than qualified to operate our business. We had worked in business and in government and in a number of cases had been in the position to give advice to "would be" entrepreneurs. We believed we knew everything we needed to know, and on the one hand, this was part the beliefs we needed to hold to have us take the leap.

As we think back, nothing was farther from the truth. You see it is one thing to know what you know, however it is an entirely different thing once you begin to understand all those things you don't know. On the surface running a business looks easy. We are told running a business is an easy equation. Sales minus expenses equals profit. Sounds easy, right? From our experience there is a lot more which goes into the equation than first meets the eye.

The analogy we use is it can be a little like making dinner only with the ingredients that are available in your kitchen. There are some people, who might look in the cupboard and find a box of Kraft Dinner. They know they have milk and butter, so this becomes a simple solution to dinner. Then there are those who look through the entire kitchen. They notice the wide range of ingredients available and from those they experiment. They throw in a little of this and a little of that. They take a little taste and then they add something else and before long, they come up with something amazing, although they would be hard pressed to ever come up with the same thing again. They haven't followed a recipe and in some cases, they have been willing to put two ingredients together which no one ever would have thought would go together, however in the end they bring uniqueness to the meal. Those people understand sometimes even though their initial concept had merit, things don't always work out as planned and there is always the chance the meal will be a flop. Does it stop them from doing what they are doing...of course not. This is the important part to remember. They move on and learn from the experience and will jump into doing the same or something new again.

The thing with the Kraft Dinner option is it increases the odds you will have a dinner you know will taste like Kraft Dinner, however we all know it doesn't guarantee it will be good. Case in point, have you ever made Kraft Dinner and it not been so good? You might have overcooked the noodles or you might have mixed the sauce poorly. While you still had noodles, it didn't get you the outcome you were looking for, yet you definitely didn't get something different. You just got lousy Kraft Dinner.

We now believe it is not about what specifically you know when you start up a business as much as what you are open to learning quickly along the way. We will tell you there have been really smart, technical people who have failed in running a business. In the fact they have been closed to learning and instead have been stuck doing the same thing over and over again...making Kraft Dinner. At the same time, there have been people who know very little about running a business, and they have gone on to great success...experimenting with ingredients. We would agree there is the chance in either case of success and we know there could be failure however there is only one option which will bring you a unique dining experience.

When people think about getting into a business there are a number of different ways to go about it. There are franchise options, there is multi-level marketing, there are professional services where you may start as a one person show, there is developing and launching a new product, there is developing new software products, there is opening a restaurant, etc. Some of these options are geared more towards the person who likes the Kraft Dinner box, and certainly there are those who will be successful with those options and in some cases very successful. They are provided with a recipe and as long as they follow it precisely, chances are they will make Kraft Dinner.

There is however a breed of people who like to create something different, and it is those we talk about who really need to be open to learning and in pursuing self development. They need to be open to knowing there is a lot they simply don't know. It is not that you are not smart enough to know it, it is just you haven't had to know it to this point. We really see learning and self development as being like the ingredients available at your disposal. Think about it like this. You can open your cupboards and see a box of Tapioca, however if you have never used Tapioca in a recipe in the past, then how would you know what you could use it for now. As soon as you understood you could use it to thicken a sauce, then it becomes another ingredient in your arsenal for making a great meal.

Like we said, there are those who have started businesses who have a lot of education and they have been trained in a profession. However they have not necessarily been trained in operating a business and for many, this is where the struggle comes in. For example, they know how to give a good massage, they know how to do a set of accounting books, they know how to put in an electrical service, however do they know anything about social media marketing or about how to finance their expansion? It is something they have to be open to learning about, if they are intending to grow their business. In our society, in some cases, we have put education and learning in a box. From this perspective, there is a belief if you want to learn something you need to go to higher education or take a business degree to start a business. According to Harvard Business School in 2009, only twenty seven out of eight hundred and eighty nine graduates went on to start their own business[ii]. That is only three percent of graduates. Now of course, some of those may go on to start a business at a later point, however at this point, an education does not seem to be the thing which drives people to start a business. For the many of you who believe you need to have an education before you start a business, change this to I need to be ready and open to learning as I go.

So what do we mean when we say you need to be open to learning? Like us, when we first started in business, we thought our learning needed to be around what we were doing, and improving how we did it. We started out consulting companies on how to increase their efficiency in their operations. We both came from technical backgrounds so for the first year of business, we continued to expand our knowledge around what we knew. We identified the trends in the industry and learned the new tools and process which were available. We attended industry trade shows and talked to people who were doing the same thing we were doing. While we were certainly doing well, before long we realized we were doing what everyone else was doing in the industry. We wanted to have more clients and soon realized we were doing the same work we had always done in our jobs, however now it was up to us to get clients and to do the work involved in figuring out how to expand our business.

At first, we did what we were doing, only harder. While we were both on Facebook, we didn't know much about social media marketing, so we disregarded it as a tool. We told ourselves it was only for connecting with friends and for young people. We fell back to advertising in the local paper, in developing our website, in bidding on projects through various bidding avenues, etc. because this is what we knew. As we said, all we did was do what we did, only with more zest. In some cases it added some work although we found it took up a lot of time and energy.

It was actually a conversation with my son, which had us think about things a little differently. He was telling me about how a local sports team he was on was doing a fundraising campaign, and they used Facebook as a means for generating followers and supporters. It was after our conversation we were prompted to think about the question of, "How do you reach more people". Now, we know this does not seem profound however it did open us up to looking at business in a different way. You see, prior to this change in thinking, we had fallen into the trap of the conventional thinking which had us develop a marketing plan. Now, we had followed all of the convention involved in developing one. It had identified our target market, we knew who our competitors were, we knew how everyone in our industry was reaching their audience, and so we followed suit. It was a good plan however it had us doing the same old, same old.

We believe people are incredible problem solvers if they get clear on what they are solving. The thing is we spend much of our time applying the same solutions over and over again without really understanding what we are working to solve. The difference between good business leaders and great ones are whether or not they are pushing themselves to solve bigger problems in different ways. In our case, we didn't know much about social media so even in developing our wonderful marketing plan; it wasn't something we even saw as an ingredient. It was like the Tapioca. Again, you can't know what you don't know.

If you look at our marketing plan today, versus what it was when we started it is different, however it wouldn't have been if we had closed ourselves off to learning. The conversation with my son had me be curious and the moment this happened, we became open to something else.

If you are thinking about getting into business or are wanting to grow your business, then you have to be CURIOUS. You have to be prepared to learn lots about a lot of different things. Those around you can be more than willing to tell you what you want to know, however you need to be prepared to ask the questions. In our case, we started looking for information on how do you grow a list and we found there was social media advertising, there was customer referral programs, there was being nominated for awards, there was writing books, etc. There are lots of different ways of growing your list, however it will require you to do something different.

From our experience, push yourself to open up your thinking in a different way. With the internet, it is easy to find solutions and answers however you need to be prepared to get clear on what you want to create and then create it. Remember some of the stuff you find, might not be applicable in this moment however from our experience it will be at some point in the future.

We had a client who was in the farming industry and we challenged him around how he could differential his business from others in his industry. He spent a lot of time telling us about what his competitors were doing and while they were good ideas, they simply made him the same. We asked him if he was prepared to do something different and he agreed. We had him attend a medical device conference. At first he didn't think it made a lot of sense however he agreed to go. When he came back he was full of a bunch of different ideas of how he could apply some of the information he obtained into his own business and it made a huge difference in his growth. He was open to learning in a different way.

While it is important to remain current with your product or service and what it has to offer, it is equally if not more important to keep up with expanding your own thinking about what is happening in the business world, with technology, with industry and government. We will say, if you are someone who doesn't like to learn new things then being an entrepreneur might not be for you depending on the size and type of business you intend to run. If you are someone who only takes advantage of learning which is presented to you on a silver platter, then again being an entrepreneur might not be for you. If you want someone to tell you everything you need to do, and in some cases even how to do it, then know it would probably be easier to be an employee.

You must be CURIOUS and you must embrace the idea that in few cases, there is a box of Kraft Dinner when you decide to get into business. Most often you will need to be willing to take the leap to create a different kind of meal knowing it might be a flop, however in the process you will get better and better at doing what you are doing as you learn. The more ingredients you have the more flexibility you will have when it comes to putting it all together.

KNOW WHAT YOUR WORTH

Let us ask you, "Do you understand what you are worth?" Do you really know? If you don't know what you are worth, how will anyone else? In order for you to remain viable as a business, this is such a critical question. At the same time, this is probably the most difficult question to answer at times as an entrepreneur.

From a young age, people are engrained in a personal worth scenario based on what they do per unit of time. As a young person, you start looking for your first job and let's say it pays you twelve dollars an hour. The moment you accept the job, in that moment you become worth what that job pays you. You accept the worth or value proposition of the situation as part of who you are, and you begin to believe this is what you are worth. Sure as you gain experience over time, you may believe you are worth a little more however it is not like suddenly you believe you are worth a thousand dollars an hour. To understand what you are worth, you may compare yourself to others who are doing the same thing you are doing, and you will hold a belief about whether you are being paid appropriately in comparison. However it is not like suddenly you believe you are worth a thousand dollars an hour. Even if you get a promotion, you accept the position and terms based on what the company has defined for the position and again in the acceptance, you now have a new basis for what you are worth. This is how people define their worth however what we will ask is, "Who says?" Why is your worth relative to someone else? Why is it some hairdressers make thirty five dollars a haircut and others make five thousand? Is it that they have special shampoo? Is it that they have magical scissors? What is the difference, because after all, it is still a haircut?

Of course, we understand organizations think in terms of the value a single person will add to the company and it is why they have wage structures. They consider what other organizations are paying for the same types of employees and you will hear them say, "We pay competitive wages." So what does this have to do with you and your business?

It comes down to value, or perceived value, both for you inside your company and outside. Some questions to think about are: How does what you do add value in your business? How do you communicate the value you add as a business to your customers and clients? How is it you differentiate yourself from your competitors through your value proposition?

Let's look at the first one: How does what you do add value in your business? We know if you are in business you may say you do many important things. You are correct, we know many business owners who like to do everything they can themselves in order to keep their costs down. They believe it doesn't cost anything when they do it. Before we go further, consider what does this say about their mindset in terms of their own value to their company? What about the lost opportunity working "in" rather than, "on" their business? Are there situations it would make better sense to hire out? Would holding this thinking push you to increase your value?

For example, we worked with a business owner who was spending time doing service calls as his team was not able to keep up with the demand. His company billing rate was sixty dollars an hour and he was spending approximately thirty hours per week in the field. When we asked him how much it was costing him, he answered, "Right now I'm saving money because I don't have to pay another person". We laughed and asked in response, "How much is it costing you in both time and lost opportunity?" He didn't have a response so we asked, "What are you worth per hour?" His answer was, "Forty dollars an hour based on how much I pay myself." We asked, "How much is your service vehicle per hour?" To which he replied, "Sixteen dollars an hour". "How much is your overhead?" we asked. "Twelve dollars per billable hour", he said. Now under normal circumstance, he had a twenty percent margin on his sixty dollar hourly charge hour rate or a profit of twelve dollars per hour. Was he saving money or was it costing money to have him cover his service calls? Considering he generally paid his employees approximately twenty dollars an hour and he was double that, in fact losing money. When we pointed out to him that for every hour he was making a service call, he was losing money because he could have someone else at half the price doing the work, at first he disagreed. He believed because he was already getting paid, it didn't matter if he was making service calls and it was better than sitting around the office. In this moment, he wasn't focused on growing, he was focused on sustaining his business. He was comfortable making service calls, because after all this is what he knew. When we asked him how much time he was spending on getting new contracts and increasing his value proposition, he admitted it wasn't a whole lot because he was busy making service calls. Suddenly he got the point realizing he didn't really know how to go after other markets and wasn't all that comfortable around it. We helped him to change his focus and to continue to grow his business. This is, once he let go of his need to work "in" his company and moved to working "on" his company.

Now, let's look at the second one; How do you communicate the value you add as a business to your customers and clients? Some people say market dictates price. To this we agree to an extent, but to this we ask, why do some lawyers charge double, triple or even quadruple what others do in the same geographical location? Why do some plumbers charge more than others? If the market was the sole indicator of price, would all examples of product or service not command the same price? The answer is no.

This difference comes down to how you add value in what you are doing. In the case of the lawyer, there are some that have more experience, there are some who are willing to take on harder cases and are prepared to risk a loss to charge a higher rate. There are some who have built themselves as an expert by doing things outside of being a lawyer such as speaking at conferences. Is the work they do any different or is it they have established a higher sense of self worth, understanding they may lose some clients or customers?

If you were to implement a twenty percent increase to your rates tomorrow what would happen to your client base? Would it drop? Most fear it will, so they hold tight. Recently, we worked with a hair stylist and you would think this would be a set market with set market rates, wouldn't you. Over a period of about six months, she increased her rates in excess of twenty five percent, and to her amazement she never lost a client. Simply, her clients valued her more than she valued herself, and her relationship with them was more valuable than the industry standard. Overnight she added to her worth, and she continues to expand her thinking and her client base. You see, when you value what you do and provide great value to your clients and customers, they want to come to you.

What is value to one, may or may not be value to another and you need to be prepared for this. What is it specifically that equates to value? If you consider an industry, there are those who demand more value from a service, and those are the ones who are generally willing to pay more. What does this greater value equate too for this person? We ask you what is your value proposition, that is, what are you worth? In order to be a viable business, you must be adding value somewhere. No one else can tell you what it is for you as an entrepreneur, you need to find a way to understand it for yourself.

Consider this, we have come to you with a business case to grow your revenue and profit margin in your business. We let you know up front we are going to charge you at a rate of a thousand dollars per hour, and we estimate it will take our team one hundred hours to complete the project. We have a notion you may say it is too expensive because most small business owners do. To which we would literally ask, in comparison to what value proposition? If you are comparing it to the cost of a haircut, sure this would be expensive. However, consider with the information we have provided you, how would you know if it is expensive or if it is valuable for that matter? Is it the rate? Is it the total charge of potentially one hundred thousand dollars? At this point, how could you know? You have no idea on revenue to counter the cost.

Now suppose we have a million dollar proposition for you under the same hourly rate, and number of hours. You will add one million dollars to your annual revenue stream, and you will have a twenty two percent return on that stream. Now, let us ask you, is this an expensive proposition? If you still say yes, you don't believe it is possible, or you don't understand the return on investment. If you are business minded, we are sure you would now see this would be a great investment, and for that reason you would be curious.

See in this equation, we understand our value proposition. We make you money, and you will have returns for years to come based on that increased revenue. Inside this, we understand we can charge a thousand dollars an hour because we have a proven track record in providing this kind of value. Our reputation allows us to charge what we are worth. Now, let's assume we delivered this type of return to you in year one. Would you question our rate for the same opportunity again in a consecutive year? My guess is you would be more than happy to pay that kind of money again. We know our value, and can demonstrate it, so we can charge what we are worth.

Let's look at the final one; How is it you differentiate yourself from your competitors through your value proposition? What are you worth? What value are you adding to your customers or clients? Can you measure it? How do you quantify it? Do you even know? Even better yet, what are you actually charging for your time, and how are you working to increase your worth?

In your business, if you look at all the time you spend in the delivery of your product or service, do you capture it? Do you understand the cost of you working in your business? Do you understand your value working "on" your business? If you do not, we would guess you have no serious plan or strategy for growth in your company.

Like in the example of the lawyer, how are you leveraging who you are and what you know? Like we said earlier, someone is going to be considered as the expert, so why couldn't it be you and your company? What makes you the best at what you do, and are you willing to waive your own banner and tell the world who you are, or are you hanging out in the shadow, hoping someone, someday will recognize you and your company?

If you are already clear on your worth to your business, awesome, you are ahead of the curve. For those who are not, stop thinking like an employee, and realize you are no longer on the clock. If you spend your time doing hourly charge outs for your company, you are worth the return on that charge out. If this is where you are today on a daily basis, that is ok however how do you work to create new value and worth, so you change this? If you don't then you are by definition, a self employed employee. Instead of a job you can walk away from, you will have one you own, that ultimately owns you.

If you want to change those scenarios now, you need to think of yourself as if you are an entrepreneur. Think of everything as it relates to return on investment. If I put a penny out here, will it return, and how long will it take? Would that penny be better spent somewhere else? The returns you create come from your value added proposition. If you measure your worth through time alone, you will make a wage and we see this time and again. As you navigate the world of business, you will begin to see where spending your time is valuable, and where it is not. Stop spending time on those things which are not valuable and spending more time on those with higher returns.

We discussed in the last chapter the need to be attentive, and this is an area where you need to be so. It is easy to go to sleep doing the same things over and over again, however as you become aware of what you are doing, it will be easier to keep your focus on how to change it. For example, instead of telling yourself you can't afford to hire an employee, or to contract out some of the day to day stuff you are doing, what if you thought to yourself, "How can I increase my revenue to offset that cost?" Change your focus and you will change your results.

When it comes to growing your business, use those tools that will add value to your company. There are things you are good at, and things others are good at. Employ those who can help you, do your homework, and do the ones that will deliver a return for you. As an example, if you know little about online marketing, find a company that can assist you. If they are good, they can back up their claims and provide you with return information for leads, conversions, etc. Use those with expertise as an investment in growing your business.

In case we haven't been clear, it is this simple, to grow your business, stop doing and get thinking and when it seems tough, keep doing it. If you don't, know that growth will be slow, and you will run the risk of becoming obsolete. Those that stay busy working in the box are generally the last to know the world is changing around them. Drop a frog in a pot of boiling water and he will immediately jump out. Put a frog in a pot and slowly turn up the heat and he will stay there until he dies. Same scenario in business, stay busy doing in your box and one day the heat and duration of it may have you cooked.

YOU CAN'T DO EVERYTHING YOURSELF

One of the exciting things about operating a business is the variety of things which need to be done, assuming you like variety. As we have said, the learning curve can be incredibly steep as there are so many different things you can dig your teeth into. There is so much to do inside your business, in the delivery of your service and in support of these aspects. Yet, there is also an incredible number of things and ideas to explore in working on your business. As an example, if you like to be creative you can exercise your creative skills in the areas of advertising and brochure development. If you like working on computers, you can develop your own website and maybe create a blog. If you like numbers, there is the accounting that needs to be done. If you like the social aspect, there is networking and sales. In a business there really is something for everyone, and in that it is very cool.

As we discussed earlier, when you are in a job you generally do the same types of things over and over, and after a while it can get pretty boring. So especially for the first time entrepreneur, the variety involved in starting a business can be a breath of fresh air. There are so many things to look at, to understand and ultimately you are able to express a different set of skills from what you did in your previous job. You are able to take great satisfaction in accomplishing something that you didn't ever believe was possible. We know there is nothing like the feeling you get when you are learning.

The early stages of being an entrepreneur can be invigorating with all of the variety. You get to look at new ideas and work on so many new things. With this can comes that satisfaction and accomplishment of doing something you didn't believe was possible. All of this said, over time you cannot do everything yourself and really expect to grow and build your business. We have seen this over and over again in business. Business owners get in their own way of growing their businesses. Sometimes you are better off to utilize experts, contract services, or hire the expertise when it comes to doing things you are unsure of while working in your business.

In this aspect, getting into business is a little like doing a house renovation for the very first time. Have you ever spent any time watching those do it yourself renovation shows on television and thought to yourself that you would like to take on a project. On television, they make it look easy so off you go to your local building center and you get all of the materials that you will need. You check with the local expert at the store and you make sure that you are clear on what you need to do. In this, you purchase a spanking new set of tools because after all you are going to be saving money doing it yourself. You get home and you start the process of demolition and you think to yourself, "that was easy". You take a little break and you collect your thoughts. You unpack your new tools and set up all the materials, and for an instant you remind yourself what it is that you are meant to be accomplishing. You have an idea where to start, however for at least a moment, you start to second guess whether you really know enough to be doing this. You push that thought aside and you get started. You might go back and watch the show again, or read the directions, or call over a buddy to give you some help, however you do get started and maybe for a while things are going really well. Inevitably, there will be a point, somewhere is the game when suddenly something comes up that you didn't anticipate and of course, no one mentioned that this could be a problem. You scramble for a bit because you know that in order to go on you need to solve this and depending on the type of person you are, you will either meticulously go about solving the problem, or you will be the type of person who will come up with a "work around" and hope that it will work out in the end. Unfortunately the work around often doesn't work out so well so it requires that you come back and attempt to fix it. At the end of the day you may finally get the project done, assuming you didn't give up somewhere in the middle, telling yourself you will get back to it someday. However as you add up your time, include in a factor for frustration, add up the cost of the materials and tools, and look at the end result, you question whether it would have been easier to have someone else come in and do it for you. Now we know that this doesn't happen in all cases, however you will know of an example where this has happened to you. We all have had these.

For the new entrepreneur, sometimes this type of thing can become an issue. You have seen a lot of different people do various things over the years and with the internet it is easy to get instructions on how to do pretty much everything. There are tutorials for this and instructions for that, so it can be easy to learn to do pretty much anything. Many believe they can do it all and do not recognize every hour they are spending doing something that is not generating sales is taking away from growing their business.

Now here comes the balancing act. There are things which certainly may make sense for you to do in starting your business, however you need to be aware of what it will cost you to have someone with more expertise do it. Let us give you a personal example. One of the things we like to do is to send out thank you cards to the people around us that make life a little easier. It is a great way so show gratitude and it is a way to keep in contact with people. It reminds them that you are around and that you appreciate their support. When we first started, we purchased a bunch of blank cards because we wanted to customize them to our company. We would just use our printer to print them, whenever we needed them. Sure it took some time at the front end to set things up however it seemed more personal in doing it ourselves. They looked great and it was a fun challenge in being able to do something like this. In fact in doing this, we next designed our own brochures and pamphlets because in our minds it would be expensive to have someone else do this.

One day our printer broke down and when we got our new one, it was significantly different from the one we had before. We were going to have to do a whole new redesign on the cards and brochures in order to print them. I started on the process of doing this, however at the same time we had a number of tight deadlines that were coming up. It was late one night when I started trying to reformat the cards and after a couple of hours, I got really frustrated because it was taking far longer than I thought it would take and at the end of it, I didn't seem to be any further ahead. In an instant, I sent off an email to a friend of mine who was in the printing industry with a concept of what I wanted on the cover and went home for the night. The next morning she replied to me with a picture of what the card would look like and told me that for one hundred cards and envelopes it would cost me one hundred and five dollars. We were shocked. There was no doubt that it was costing us far more than a dollar fifty a card when you factored in our time for setup, our time to print and the cost of supplies without even remotely considering the loss of revenue as a result of my time being used doing this. It was an eye opener for us.

Please be clear, there will definitely be things in your business you will be able to do. The question is whether it makes sense for you to do them? Let's say you start up a legal firm and you charge yourself out at three hundred dollars an hour. Then for every hour you work servicing clients you make three hundred dollars. Now if you are also the one typing letters, chances are you could find someone at twenty dollars an hour to do this, freeing you up to take on additional clients for more money. This may have been an obvious example however you need to not only know what you are worth. You need to know what other services are worth and you constantly need to be weighing and balancing these.

The second thing to consider is can you really do it as well as someone who is in the business of that service? You know yourself when you are skilled in doing something you know where the short cuts are. In the case of the do it yourself renovation, a professional doesn't have to think about what the first step is. They already know how to use the tools and chances are they have already figured out how to deal with the challenges that come up in doing that kind of work. Sure they may charge you more to get the job done, although generally speaking they will do it in far less time than you. They will more than likely do a better job and let's admit it, the job will be done and you will be able to move on.

We run into a lot of entrepreneurs that have a huge list of things that have to be done. There are some things on the list which are really important, there are things on the list they like to do, and then there are things on the list that will provide little return to the business in general. It is human nature to tackle the things which are either easier to do or you like to do. The problem exists when you leave the important stuff because you are tied up in those other things. For example, if you don't like to network it is easy to hide behind all the stuff you tell yourself you need to do however is what you are doing really growing your business? You need to be honest with yourself. If there is something you don't like to do which is important, then we tell our clients do it over and over again until you do like it. Find a way to build it into something you like to do. The only reason you don't like doing something is because you don't feel accomplished in doing it. You don't feel you are getting the results you would like to have so you avoid it. The simple truth is the more you do something the better you get at it and if you want to run a successful business you need to get good at doing the things which will make you money.

Especially during the start-up phase, money can be tight, so it is easy to fall into doing everything yourself. You discount your time and effort and believe that you are not costing you anything. Nothing could be further from the truth. Use your time and resources wisely and be clear that the more you are working in your business, the less you are working on your business.

As your business grows, the next step will be to constantly review what it is you are doing. Any business will become maxed out based on its resources. If you want to grow beyond a start up, you need to constantly be aware of what tasks you are doing. You need to avoid going to sleep on this. Just because you were the one doing the books from the start, could you be charging yourself out to clients and paying someone else to do them? Just because you are the one who makes the follow up calls to your clients to ensure that they remember their appointments, what would it cost to have someone else do it? This does not necessarily mean adding employees, initially. There are a lot of different businesses that would be more than happy to assist you in doing the things which are not bringing you value, however you need to be prepared to get out there and find out what they truly cost and then seriously evaluate this against what it costing you. Remember you can always change your mind later if it is not working, but you will never know until you give it a try....you might find they do it better than you.

YOUR BOOK SMART IS KILLING YOUR STREET SMART

How smart are you? We know there are many ways you could attempt to quantify this however, really, how smart are you? In society you hear people talk about other people, even pets for that matter, in terms of how smart (or the opposite, how stupid) they are, but have you ever really thought about what this means? It could mean:

How much education do they have…certificates, degrees, etc.
The ability to regurgitate or remember information.
The ability to apply what they know.
The ability to adapt in changing situations.
The job or type of job they have.
The ability to solve problems.
How successful someone is or how much money they have.

We hazard to guess you have selected some variation of the above, however, we ask you, what is smart? When you think about it, smart is such a generalization.   When we see someone around us accomplish something which maybe we don't believe we could do, we chalk it up to them being smart. When someone provides us with a thought which hadn't occurred to us, we chalk that up to them being smart. When we hear about someone who has a big position or who has obtained a lot of degrees, we chalk them up to being smart, however smart is really hard to quantify. There will be moments when you have felt smart and other times when not so much. We all do.

From our perspective, we believe smart is about the ability for someone to think beyond the circumstances, present right here, right now. Some may consider this to be problem solving or being able to apply information. In some ways this applies, however we take it a step further because we believe it comes down to being able to think beyond the convention of group think.

So what do we mean when we say the "convention of group think"? From the time when we are young, we are told there are rules about how to do things. In school, we are taught rules and when to use them. Those who are able to regurgitate that information and apply those rules are the ones who do well.

In school we are taught in a deductive versus inductive manner. In other words, we are provided with an answer and then told how to get there and the reason the answer is correct. For example, Newton came up with the idea of gravity and he devised an equation to quantify it. Prior to him doing this, gravity existed however chances are there was little thought given to the idea. We are pretty sure cavemen were not concerned with this. They were probably more concerned about not being eaten by the dinosaurs. As soon as Newton put a box around it and gave it meaning, it became real and it is something we all learn about in school. Deductive thinking means you come up with a hypothesis and then you go about proving it to be correct. In fact in school, wasn't this how we did our science experiments? As soon as someone puts rules to something, it allows us in our thinking to go to sleep and never ponder whether in fact it really holds true all of the time.

We know you will agree with the fact that those in school who are able to take in the facts and data and then apply them in the box or regurgitate them on an exam do well. Let us ask you, how much do you remember about the things you were taught in school? Sure there will be some, although there will be quite a bit which you no longer have stored in your memory. Now, this is not to say you couldn't find the information if you needed it in the future. It is just because you didn't have an application for it at the time you just simply let it go from your conscious thoughts.

If you go back in history, schooling was originally meant to do a few different things. It was meant to be an avenue to transfer the rules of society. Even today in school, we are taught how to behave and the difference between right and wrong. It was meant to be an avenue to transfer knowledge, convention and history. We are taught that one plus one equals two, the Earth is part of a galaxy, and dinosaurs roamed the Earth. Finally it was meant to teach us how to follow instructions. We are taught there is a sequence to writing a story or to do accounting or to building a structure. All of these are important because you can only imagine what it would be like if we didn't have this in our society, however at the same time it can lock you up in your thinking. It has us believe there is only one answer and there is a right way and a wrong way. We know you will have seen examples where two people have different ideas about the right way to do something and yet you as an outsider, recognize either one would definitely work.

Remember, to do well in school you had to be book smart. The premise of this being "don't question, it just is, learn it, follow instructions and repeat". By the time you graduate you are well conditioned to the social system. Take in information and follow the instructions. Now if you go and demonstrate your ability to take in information and follow instructions diligently through advanced education, you are then granted permission or the rights and privileges to perform some task in the world.

Please understand, we say this tongue and cheek as we fully acknowledge our own educational backgrounds. We do respect the institution of education and because of this we appreciate the benefits and at the same time recognize the limitations especially for the entrepreneur in creating something outside of the norm. You will agree there are people who have a lot of education who know little beyond what the book says and at the same time there are people who have little education and go on to create amazing things.

Now as a premise, learning rules and convention might be a good thing if it were a fact they are always true, however they are not. There was a time when the world was believed to be flat. There was a time when asbestos was considered a wonder product. There was a time when it was believed there was only one galaxy. There was a time when it was believed no one would be able to afford or have the space to own a computer. Something which is fact today can simply be a fallacy tomorrow.

It is human nature to think deductively. This deductive thinking gives us rules and the rules give us certainty. We like to come up with a hypothesis and then go prove it to be true. If you can prove it then it is true and if you can't, then reform it and try again. If you have ever done any work with statistics you will know this is true. While many people think data must be true, there are a lot of different ways to bend the truth. The fact of the matter is most people are unaware of how they think and operate so they simply rely on the thinking of someone else and never question the intention behind what they are being told.

To understand this, take for example your neural capabilities. For purpose of explanation, consider yourself as a machine, and your ability to measure your environment is through your five senses; olfactory (smell), gustatory (taste), auditory (hearing), visual (seeing), and kinesthetic (feeling). Each of these areas has settings, specific to you and how you operate in your environment. This means you are picking up different information from those around you. The information you pick up is relayed through your neural processing unit, however you will agree in some cases you may be missing information that others pick up. For a moment, just think about a situation where you describe it one way and someone else describes it differently. It happens all the time. You are programmed to pick up certain information based on your own unique belief system and that belief system is heavily influenced by the "convention of group think". The more a group thinks in a certain way, the more it becomes real.

If you believe there is a right way to do something then you will notice when someone else is either doing it right or doing it wrong. For years, there was a belief that being left handed was a bad thing. Parents and teachers of children who were left handed were constantly reminding them to use their right hand and to fit in. If you were left handed you probably found this annoying and if you were right handed, you would have thought yourself to be "normal". Being left handed was seen as a disability not because it was, but because there was a "convention of group think". If you were the guys selling the "cure" to being left handed, then you would have seen this convention as being helpful to your cause…to make more money. Can you think beyond the convention and who is benefiting from it existing?

Now back to smart. The question we ask is whether your book smart is killing your street smart? We know in business there is a lot of conventional thinking. Like we talked about earlier, you can get caught up in thinking that you have to charge market rates for your services. If you have gone to business school, you will know you must have a business plan and a marketing plan before you do anything. You may believe you shouldn't have any debt. We know in some cases, each of these could be true however they do not apply to all and in some cases they apply to none.

Let's give you an example of this. Increasingly over the last decade you hear more and more about there being an increase in Attention Deficit Disorder (ADD), and Attention Deficit Hyperactivity Disorder (ADHD) in individuals. The education system has struggled to put in systems to have these kids retain information and follow instructions, and there is a focus on addressing this through the use of drug treatments. This has become a real problem.

ADD and/or ADHD are often characterized as a mental disorder and a neurobehavioral disorder characterized by either significant difficulties of inattention or hyperactivity and impulsiveness or a combination of the two.[iii] What this means is the individual struggles to hold the attention span required in the traditional educational setting to learn material and therefore lacks the ability to follow instructions. To hear about this, you might believe it is problem, however what if it wasn't? In fact, we believe this a wonderful adaption of the human species to realign the individual to the inherent function of thinking. Through the difficulties of processing in classroom information, the person has to develop thinking strategies rather than follow direction strategies.

When we said, what if this were not a problem? Consider this. People who are considered to have ADD or ADHD are 300% more likely to start their own business [iv] as compared to non diagnosed kids and adults. Just to demonstrate here is a large list of business leaders who are considered to have ADHD;

Richard Branson, founder of Virgin Airlines

John T. Chambers, CEO of Cisco Systems

Ingvar Kamprad, Swedish founder and chairman of IKEA Stores

David Neeleman founder and CEO of Jet Blue Airways

Charles Schwab the founder, chairperson, and CEO of the Charles Schwab Corporation, the largest brokerage firm in the U.S.

Perhaps one of the greatest twists in the increasing diagnosis rates of ADHD is there will be an upsurge in entrepreneurship in the coming decades. These personality types are known for taking their own path because they don't seem to fit into the traditional system and therefore have a tendency to reject the "convention of group think".

In order to be an entrepreneur, you need to think like an entrepreneur. You have to be able to think beyond what you have in front of you, or you will become paralyzed or you will do the same things over and over again hoping for a different result. One of our favorite questions is "Who Says?" We will tell you it is those who understand the rules and yet are willing to push up against the convention are the ones who create something different.

We will tell you first hand, what you learn in books does not always apply. We worked with an individual who had a degree in business. When she got into business, she wrote a wonderful business plan and on paper it looked amazing. Unfortunately, business wasn't doing so well so she tweaked her plan to better represent the reality she was experiencing. At this point she came to see us, we asked her what she intended to do differently and she was able to tell us what it was she had been taught to do. We asked if she had done this and she said she had however it was obvious it wasn't working. At some point, she needed to let go of what the books said and to think through different options, to think what this meant to her and her own situation. As soon as she let go of the convention then it freed her up to make some amazing changes in her business.

Highly successful people have a trait in common. They plan out their idea, make a decision quickly and hold to the idea over time. Those who are less accomplished tend to be slow in making decisions and change their mind often. Which are you? We know for a fact, you will gather as much information as you have time to collect and will never have enough information to proceed until the point you need to make a decision. We know only one thing can grow your business and it is your ability to think beyond what everybody sees as limitations.   Consider this.   What is the difference between two entrepreneurs in the same business?   It is not in what they do, it is in how they think about what they do.   How is it Sir Richard Branson can go into the airline industry when everyone said he was crazy and create Virgin Airlines and make it incredibly successful and yet others are dealing with failing airlines?   The difference is in how he thought about the opportunity and his commitment around making it happen.

The late Steve Jobs said in his recently published biography, "I began to realize that an intuitive understanding and consciousness was more significant than abstract thinking and intellectual logical analysis."   He also said that, "intuition is a very powerful thing, more powerful than intellect, in my opinion.   That's had a big impact on my work."   We talk more about this thinking in our first book, "It Is What It Is, or Is It.... All About Business".   Increase your intuition and trust of self, and you will increase your street smarts.   After all, there is only you at the end of the day and you are worth investing in to push your thinking. You invested in your business so understand you also need to make an investment in you.

FRIENDS AND FAMILY DON'T BUY

For many entrepreneurs, there simply can't be enough said about our friends and family in their support of us. We will tell people, they are an amazing support system and you should appreciate everything they do and will do for you in creating your dream of running a business. These are the people who will be up with you all night packaging product for sale. They will put on their aprons when you decide you want to have a launch barbeque and will never say a word as they are covered with grease and smell like hot dogs. They will be the ones who you will call on when you need to assemble your store fixtures or to paint your store. There is not one entrepreneur who wouldn't at the end of the day say they have achieved what they have achieved because of these amazing people. They are your own set of cheer leaders, however at the end of the day, and please listen.....they don't buy from you.

I know this might seem a little startling to most people, however it really is the truth. It is not that they don't support you and it is not that they don't want you to do well. It really comes down to two things. On one side, they don't want to crush your dreams so in the moment you talk about going into business, they will sincerely be telling you what you want to hear to support you. The second issue comes down to whether you will ever really be able to charge them, considering everything that they do for you.

If you are like most entrepreneurs, you will have had the idea of going into business for a period of time. You will have processed a bunch of different ideas through your head and you will have talked to your friends and family about them. In some cases they may have believed you never really intended to get into business so the discussions you had, were theoretical. They may have seen it as you living a "pipe dream" because in fact they have never really considered going into business themselves. Sure, they might have given you ideas about this concept or that, however often they think why get into a disagreement around something which is not right in front of them. In those conversations, they might have even thrown out their own ideas. While you may think you are having a serious conversation, they will have seen it as just "shooting the breeze". We have talked to a lot of people who have went into business and it is funny how many times they tell us their friends and family really didn't believe it would ultimately happen.

As you get more and more settled around what it is you want to do, as an entrepreneur, you start to test the waters and of course the people you talk to are not the ones who would tell you that you are crazy. There might be a few of those, however in order for you to finally take the leap, you will have found the majority of people have found it to be a good idea. We say this is a little like a company asking for references for a perspective employee. As you will agree, when you need to give a reference, it is not like you give a name of someone who you haven't had a good working relationship with. You provide the names of people who like you. The same goes for asking people what they think about your new business idea. You will be asking people who know you, in what you do and of course because they like you, they will tell you they can see you being successful in taking on your new venture. Of course this is what you want to hear. If you couldn't see yourself starting a new business, you wouldn't be asking the question. If you are honest even in those moments someone may have told you something you didn't want to hear, but you will have defended yourself and your abilities to be successful. As a result, you might have even adjusted some of your thinking related to what they said, however you will have heard what you wanted to hear. This is simply human nature, considering the dials on your processing unit as we discussed earlier.

The minute you decide on the business you are going to start you put the wheels in motion, you start to tell your family and friends about your new venture. Remember they want to support you, so they tell you things like:

I think that is a great idea. I'll buy from you.

I know a friend who could really use your services. I'll let them know what you are doing.

Let me know when you are going to open and I will be there.

That is wonderful we will have that service available, I am so looking forward to booking an appointment.

Awesome, I don't like the person I am dealing with now and will love coming to you.

Let me know when you get started and we will have a chat.

The list will go on and on. Of course you like to hear this because it supports your idea. In the moment you may in fact believe them because they are your friends, family and business associates. You have a relationship where they have always been honest with you and their sincerity in the moment really will be genuine. We have heard examples of this over and over again, and the new business owner is often shocked when these offers do not come to fruition.

So why is it that this ultimately doesn't occur? Well for one, if these individuals are currently using a service or buying a specific product it is difficult to move to something else. Business is about relationships and while they may have a great one with you, there will be comfort for them in what they know. For example, if they have gone to a hairdresser for a long period of time, even though they know you will do a good job, right now they don't have to think about "training" someone new in what they like. As a printing company, you can think of it this way for example. If someone is currently already employing a printing service, then to make a switch, they would have to re-engage in something different. This seems simple enough, however think of this, you know you are a creature of habit and so are the people around you. We generally buy groceries at the same place, buy clothing at the same place, and have our taxes done at the same place. We do most of the things we do over and over from the same place in the same manner. It makes life simple to have that kind of certainty and so it generally needs to be really compelling for us to move. Either we need to become unsatisfied in feeling pain in the current service, or the deal on the other side needs to be of greater value. Unfortunately sometimes you just being you isn't always enough to garner the switch to you as a provider.

The second thing that can occur is if they are your friends, family or business associates, they will expect you will give them a "deal" on what you are offering. If you are doing something you love to do, it could be you have done it for free and now you decide you want to create a business around it. In some cases this might be an option however in setting your prices, you will have generally set those based on market pricing and the value you are providing. You will know what your competitors are charging and how you have differentiated yourself from them. While you may decide to give a discount you will also be aware you are, for example giving them the product or service at your cost. If you do too much of this then of course it is eating into your viability as a business. Sure you may purchase an item at twenty dollars and may choose to sell it at your cost, however often for the new entrepreneur costs associated with operating their business are not realized in the selling at cost. The result, selling below actual cost. Think of it this way, you have the cost of running the operation, the cost of paying yourself, the cost of your office, the cost of training and education and financing your business. All of this overhead needs to be factored in to your product cost. When this cost isn't factored in making the earlier deal, you are in fact losing money selling to your close network. It won't take long before you are out of business and while they might be happy in the moment, you will be miserable in the long run.

This feeds into the next factor and that one is you. Especially during start up, your family and friends do so much to help you, and you will feel a need to pay them back for all they do, somehow. You will want to give away anything you can in an attempt to pay them back and this will play with your psyche. Please recognize you need to act now as you plan to go forward. At some point, just know you will feel you have adequately paid them back for what they have given you and when that point happens, you will start to see things differently. On your side, if you make a "deal" at some point you will want to change the arrangement that you have in place. At the same time, you will feel you are locked into a commitment that will go on forever.

We worked with an electrician, who was incredibly grateful for the support he received from his friends during the start up of his company. He agreed to do electrical work for the cost of the supplies in order to pay them back. Over a period of time he provided a lot of free services and before long it became somewhat of an expectation. Anytime someone needed a plug or a fixture to be installed he got the call. After a while, he recognized for every hour he was spending doing these kinds of things, he was also missing out on work which would have paid him well. You can imagine there was a lot of conflict within him to change the situation. After a while, he decided to let his friends know if they needed work done, he would be putting it through the company and he would give them an estimate for the work they needed done. In some cases, his friends understood and continued to use his services. In other cases, they decided that some of the things they were getting him to do, they could do themselves and in other cases, it ultimately ended up impacting their friendships in a negative way. You see a lot of times our friends and family are not really aware of what we are worth. In this case, sure they understood what an electrician got paid per hour however they didn't know what the company charge per hour was worth. They were fine paying him as an employee however they didn't think they should have to pay him with all the overhead and expense associated with the running of a company. From his perspective, why would he give up work which would pay his company rate, in order to continue to pay a debt that he felt was more than paid?

In terms of your psyche, you know how much your products or services are worth and you need to be prepared to own that. If you get into the cycle of discounting, it is easy to fall into the trap of always believing you need to discount. The longer you are in business the better you will get to know your clients and customers and in some cases, they may become your friends. If you are discounting for one, before long you will be discounting for many and it becomes difficult to stop. Know your market and how much you are worth and be prepared to hear "no". We always say the more "no" you get out of the way, the more "yes" you can get to. If someone doesn't want your product or service for the price you are charging, evaluate it in terms of the whole rather than on specific relationships.

Now certainly we believe there will be those friends, family and associates who will use your services and buy your products however our advice would be not to count on them in planning out your business. Know you are going to have to do the work to get new clients and customers. We always consider family and friends as "gravy" when it comes to operating a business. If you go in not relying on them, then you will have the flexibility to do what makes sense over the long haul, however if you go in with them being a substantial portion of your revenue, then that is when things get far more difficult.

We know without a doubt your friends and family mean the world to you and we also know they care about you and they want to see you succeed. They are there because they want to be part of your success and chances are they are asking little in return. Thank them in different ways. Take them for lunch, host a thank you barbeque, buy them tickets to a show. Do something which means something to them and know if they really want to come to you, it is because it is you and not because they are getting a deal.

YOU CAN BE CERTAIN FLIP FLOPPING IS JUST FLEXIBILITY

So, you are starting a new business or working in your business, and you know the right way to do things, correct? When we started in business, we did too. We knew the things we knew, and we knew the right way to do them. We set out on a path and we did them, very well we might add. We added new clients and experienced new growth. What we didn't initially anticipate was this growth brought in the need for change in how we did things. We hadn't factored in the human individuality equation.

To frame this, let us go back to the onset of our company. We initially set on a course of consulting to companies in processes we knew how to do. We were resident experts so to speak. As we navigated these many companies, we noticed many different companies with different individuals. The key here being, individuals. People are the common denominator in any business or company, and we do see them as individuals. After all, we are all different and we like to be treated that way. People love to put their spin and individuality into anything they do. As part of this, we had to learn how to be flexible in how we implemented process and ideas to create performance. What worked well for one company or individual may not for another. You have seen the blanket programs, if they worked, would all companies not benefit from a standard implementation?

While we like to see people as people, we also recognize within any company there is a way in which things are done which is unique to that company and the people who work there. You have seen this, we are sure. You enter a new work place and people tell you how things are. They tell you how they do things and will tell you, "This has always been done this way". Perhaps you do this or see this in your business now. You operate a certain way and you tell everyone how things are done. You know the way it is and the way you need to do it. After all, you know your world and how it operates. How could someone new or someone who doesn't know, know something better? Every day you do what you do.

We like to call this being "certain" in your world. Traditionally, people are drawn to certainty. They like to know what they know, to know what they do, and they tend to like to keep things certain and done a certain way. The idea of inserting new ideas or ways of doing things will always bring something into question, and this uncertainty can be unpalatable for some. It brings with it the discomfort of, "what if this happens, or what if that happens". The reality is certainty negates the need to think in the world. This in mind, people generally don't like to rock the boat. You know if you do something a certain way, you will get a certain outcome so you have a tendency to "check your brain" and just do the process.

Now when we go into a company, we typically see three categories of people within every organization. There are those who are completely closed to change, those arrested, and those who are open to and embrace change. We know you will know people in each of these categories. The obvious is, those open to change are the most flexible and generally create the greatest results in life and business. You may even have an idea of where you are today. Before you decide, be *open* to what we have to say.

You have met those who are closed, in they are unwilling to effect any change from the norm. For these individuals, often if someone wants to change something, they will interpret it as evil. They may even feel their job will be to expose the evil sources in their organization. The people who ask the question "Why are we doing it this way? I know we could make it better." are the ones who they see as being evil. For someone who is closed, when change is proposed, this brings about anxiety and fear. We do things the way we do them because we have always done them this way, and as far as they are concerned they always will. Any type of uncertainty will completely unsettle these individuals. If a process fails which has worked in the past, they will say, "Next time we just need to do it better." They will see the failure as a freak accident and even if something did change, they will ignore the fact and continue to want to do it the same old way. In fact any time something doesn't work in the organization, the fallback position is do it better, pay better attention to the details, or do it harder and it will work. Now, please don't mistake these individuals as lazy. In fact, in many cases they are some of the hardest workers in an organization. It takes a tremendous amount of work to constantly try to do something over and over again when it is not working or when it isn't yielding the results it once did. Often we associate this mindset with the long term employee or the older generation, however this is not necessarily the case.

The closed group is easy to work with because they are easy to identify. To work with the group as you introduce change, show them the similarities between what they are doing and what they were doing. Show them how they can get a new result in the same vein of thinking. In their mind, they can only see the differences when it comes to change and these differences hold all of the uncertainties in world. Show them the similarities, so they can see how they will be doing something the same.

The next group is the arrested group. The arrested group is the most dangerous because they are generally disengaged and less interested in working to get a solution. This is the group of people who like to blame others when something doesn't go right. They will say things like, "I just did what I was told to do" or "I knew it wouldn't work, but no one asked me for my opinion". For anyone working to make change in an organization, this type of person can be frustrating because on the surface it can feel like they are intentionally sabotaging the larger group efforts.

In reality, while certainly they maybe sabotaging, for the most part, they just want to be left alone. In a workforce, these are the people who have retired on the job and are just counting down the days until they in fact retire off the job. They will do the minimal amount of work to stay employed and find themselves just going through the motions each and every day. This group is the most dangerous because they are stuck. At least with the close group, they have an opinion and are willing to fight for what they believe in. They have a conviction and as you move them in a new way of thinking, they will have equally as much conviction around that. With the arrested group, they will do whatever they have been told to do, however they simply "check their brains" so the entire organization suffers from the benefit it could achieve if the person were engaged.

In this case, it is how flexible you are in re-engaging them in something they can have their own individual success in. A lot of times, people fall into this group when they have not been allowed to be their own individual or when they have come to realize that regardless of what they do, they will be recognized the same as everybody else, whether that is in compensation or recognition. The key to moving these people is in the combination of patience and pressure. You need to apply pressure in order to have them move and you need to realize initially, it will be slow going, however as you reward them for re-engaging, they can become a valuable contributor to the organization. They have generally seen it all and they will have great ideas on how it can be different. People in this group believe they have been "written off" so at first the idea that someone could believe in them and would want their ideas can be a little unbelievable to them. They may even test your commitment to what you are saying and thus the need for patience is critical. In our experience, they always come around if you stick with them.

Now, the open group to you may seem obvious. They are open to change. Please understand there are those who make change, just to make change and then there are those who make change when it makes sense. We believe that great entrepreneurs are the later. They are quick and responsive. They are quick to see when something is not working any longer and to make adjustments. Some may even break it initially in order to make it better. From the outside, they can appear to be flip floppy, to someone who is either closed or arrested. These are the ones who create chaos and uncertainty for the other two groups.

Now, where are you in the world? Be open and honest with yourself. It is the only way you can change it. The best way to know is to listen to what you say to the world. Do you talk about the right way? Do you refer to the operations manual? Do you want to save people from themselves? What do you do?

Part of the challenge in determining where you are, is you do not live in one group all of the time. Maybe at home you are really open and yet when you get to work you are arrested. Maybe when you get around your family you are closed and yet when you are learning something new you are open. Now, in good times, you may be completely open, however where do you go when the shit hits the fan? We mean when things get bad. What do you say to yourself? Do you get stuck in the right way? Do you get emotionally charged and hold your idea? We say, let your emotions be your guide. If you feel some sort of emotional charge one way or another, you are invested in your thinking. If you are invested in your thinking, you are not open. It is only when you are free of any emotional charge one way or another that you can be free to be open.

Would you agree the world is changing? Would you agree we are seeing technological advancements at a pace we have never seen previously? Yet in some areas, we have seen little change. Human nature is to do what you do, and do it until you exist no more.

Think about this, if Henry Ford had been stuck in the right way and the way everybody knew of doing things, would his vision of improved travel have been to figure out how to get "faster horses"? If the Wright Brothers were stuck in what everybody knew, would they have been the first to fly? If Steve Jobs believed bigger was better would a room full of computing power in the 1970s be sitting in your handheld device today? You have to be open, especially as an entrepreneur if you want to create something different. Like we said earlier, you need to be curious.

How charged are you on what you are doing? Can you change openly under changing conditions? See, the world typically type casts and rejects those who change their minds quickly in changing situations. They see them as flip floppers. It was Arthur Schopenhauer, an influential philosopher in the nineteenth century, who wrote about truth and ideas and how they go through three stages. In the first stage, they are ridiculed. In the second stage, they are violently rejected, and in the third stage they are finally considered self evident. In this third stage things finally become evident or imminent.

If you are to truly capitalize on your industry or market as a business owner or entrepreneur, open your mind. Open your thinking. You must be open to change, however to do this you need to change your thinking and you need to be pushed in your thinking. Understand, it's only your ideas of what you believe now that have you be arrested or closed to something new. Make the commitment, anytime you hold an emotional charge on how to do something to ask yourself, "Is this my need to be right? Is it that I am right or is it I believe that I need to be right?" Be open to something different and know you will find an answer which is right in that moment. I know you will agree with us as you look around, there are more and more people telling each other what to do, how to behave, what is right and what is wrong. In some cases we are even legislating in beliefs to create laws. Think of abortion as a topic around the world. Some would say we are taking away what it means to be an individual who is free to change their mind in changing conditions. Be prepared that moments change and so do the right answers. In our work, we have found most people think they are open, however relatively few truly are. Even the most closed minds will look out at the world and point out the closed minds of the world. It is easy to see it in others. The magic comes when you can recognize it in yourself and when you make the choice to change it. The results and success driven individuals in business thrive to lead. It is in this very nature they remain open.

START UP BUDGET TIMES IT BY THREE

We have assisted a number of business people after they have decided to get into business, and the one challenge they generally face is they didn't plan for the unexpected and ultimately they run into cash problems. In some cases, the business will fail even before it gets a chance to succeed. This is generally one of the top ten reasons why a start up business will fail early on.

Starting up a business can be a lot like buying your first new home. For many people they focus on getting that first new home and they save and save for the down payment. As they are reaching the magical number, they engage the services of a real estate agent, they scour the real estate advertisements or they start to tour around various neighborhoods looking for the perfect home. In some cases, they go to the bank to see what they can afford and in other cases, they go out and find a home, put in the offer and suddenly they become home owners. There is the initial wave of excitement where you drive by your new home and count down the days until possession day. You knew one day you would be moving into your own place so you will have been preparing for a period of time buying furniture, pots and pans, towels, etc. In some cases, you received gifts of items from family and friends and will have plans on how you are going to set up your new home. As the move in date approaches, you start to become aware of the costs you probably hadn't anticipated although you might have been told about them. There was no way that you could have really known what it would mean when you were first being told. There is the closing fees, the taxes that need to be paid (depending on the time of the year), there is the lawyer who needs to be paid and the insurance that needs to be bought and before long, you are dipping into the funds you had planned for the renovations you had in mind. Generally at this point, it is still all good. While you are not happy about having to reallocate the funds, at the same time you are excited about your new home and you tell yourself that if you do some of the work, like doing the painting and putting down new flooring, it will all be okay and you will still have your renovations.

Moving day comes, and you get the keys to that new home and you are on top of the world. It truly is exciting. You start loading in your boxes and furniture and you realize the furnace filter needs changing, the light bulbs need to be replaced, the handle on the back door is broken, and the taps are dripping. You go out and buy the necessities you will need to live and before long the funds you had allocated for renovations are being dipped into further. You still have the dream of what you want your house to look like so you decide to stop eating out at your favorite restaurant, you start bringing lunch to work and in fact you suddenly become aware of what groceries cost. You find out that if you only eat Roman noodles, that not only can you survive, you can reallocate your budget into your house and your dream. If you were like me, you became aware of the cost of utilities and turned down the heat, let go of the extra cable packages and unplugged anything that didn't need to be plugged in regardless of how much it cost all in the attempt to create your dream house. If you hadn't guessed, this is what it means to be "house poor". If you are lucky, you manage your way through this and as a result, you certainly know better for the next time. This is part of learning and growing.

Please remember all the way through this experience there will have been people who were telling you their experience in doing the same thing, however you needed to disregard what they were saying because you thought it would be different for you. The real estate agent will have given you things like the average utilities costs, they will have warned you about closing fees, and the cost of insurance. You certainly would have listened to them, however because you hadn't ever experienced this first hand, it was hard to get your head around it. Your family and friends probably told you about their stories when they first moved into a new home, however again you would have believed you were smarter and that you would do it differently. Certainly you will have listened and taken in some of the advice they had to offer, and there will be other tidbits you totally disregarded. Please understand you need to do this, otherwise chances are you would not have made the move and you would still be living in your parent's basement.

This is the same thing when it comes to starting a business. When you start a business or if you are someone who is currently in a business, you will have had to put together in your mind what kind of sales you think you will achieve and how soon you could anticipate that happening. You will have probably done some research around this and will know what you currently know in order to have developed that. At the same time, you will have identified what you believe will be your expenses. You will have done your homework related to finding a location and about what it will cost for rent or to lease. You will have figured out the cost of fittings and administration expenses. You might have even figured out how much you want to pay yourself. In some cases, you might have attended a workshop which outlined for you how to put together a budget or financial statements. As you reflect on all you know, on the surface your idea will look like a great idea. You might have gone and talked to the bank and they will have questioned you on whether you have fully considered whether you can achieve the sales you identified or whether you believe your expenses are in line. While you will consider what they have said, you will be definite you have put together a reasonable plan. You know how much money you need and based on what you have put together it all looks good.

Notice at this point, it is the same as all your friends, family, lawyers and real estate agents trying to tell you about the cost of owning your own house. Your dream in that case was around owning your own first home and no longer living with your parents or renting an apartment. You were focused on the outcome and there was really little anyone was going to tell you, which was going to have you not fulfill that outcome. The only chance you were going to change course is if you came to it yourself.

If you watch television shows like the Dragons Den or Shark Tank, you will have seen countless numbers of people who have presented on the show with some good and some not so good ideas. One of the things which repeatedly come up as an issue is the valuation an individual has made in regards to their company. They will have placed a value of "x" amount of dollars, based on the idea that they will have future sales of "y". Over and over again, the potential investors will tell them their valuations do not make sense and because of that they "are out". You see people, who are passionate about their business proposition and who really believe it will make them a lot of money, have often invested heavily in bringing their idea to life. As a result they miss the forest for the trees. They are no longer unbiased, and they need the idea to launch more so than it is a good idea to launch. You will hear stories where people have invested their entire life saving on an idea however they now just need one more investment in order to make it take off. These ideas, most often will never take off.

Just like with your first home, you go into creating your new business with the anticipation that you will do it within your budget, however please know this rarely, if ever, happens. It always costs more than you could have anticipated. For a start-up business owner, by our experience in working with start ups, sales revenue seldom transpires the way they intended. It rarely happens that a new business goes from no sales to great sales in a month. Like in the example of a house, with the closing costs, the insurance, etc., in a new business, the owner suddenly realizes that there are things like payroll taxes, insurance, financing cost, credit card usage fees, other taxes, inventory holding costs, renovation overruns, costs in facilitating sales (time spent running your business when you yourself are not generating sales), etc. which are missed in the initial planning.

Just like in the example with your new home, when a start up business goes over budget, the owner takes action. They start to trim back on expenses, such as reducing the number of staff, bringing things like book keeping back in house, reducing operating hours, no longer allowing credit cards and in doing these things they believe if they can just hang on, then at some point it will turn around.

The difference between the business scenario and the one with the house comes down to a couple of things. Generally when you buy a house you have employment so you have a level of income that continues to come into the game even though you are pinching your pennies. As long as you are able to the pay the bills, you might not have a lot left over, however you will eventually come out the other side. In the case of a business there is not the guarantee of steady money coming in. The only money coming in is what you are generating from your sales. In the case of a business, you are forced to be focused on both sides of the equation. As you reduce your expenses, you are probably impacting your ability to generate sales. If you reduce the hours of operation, then you are impacting your ability to create sales. If you no longer take credit cards, you will be relying on people having cash thereby reducing your potential sales. Certainly there are some expenses which will have little impact on your ability to generate revenue, however, if at the front side of operating your business, you believe that what it is you were doing was important, then you have to know as you trim back on those, there will be an impact somewhere.

The second aspect which contributes to the shortage in funds is that for most new business owners, just like in the example of buying a new home, the put together a budget for what they will need to do in order to become established. They will spend a significant amount of money in developing their website, in establishing their store front, in buying equipment, etc. Many of these expenses are made even before the doors open and the money is gone. Just like in your home, there will be expenses you could never have anticipated and yet they will be important for your success. For example, you can't cut hair if you don't have a chair and scissors. These expenses are critical, however if you have spent your budget on wall paint and European designer sinks, when it is time to buy your scissors you may find you are having to dip into money which you don't really have. Once your start-up money is gone, there is no ability to maneuver and like in your home, chances are you will have under-budgeted these expenses which will ultimately cut into your buffer.

Inherently when a business starts to get in trouble, they will look for alternate means of financing and unfortunately at this point, there are few options available. They will look for small business loans, ask family and friends for money, apply for a new credit card, they will dip into their own savings or visit their bank manager all in an attempt to keep it going. The big problem at this point, they become a bad business risk or at least appear this way. People look at them and think, you have already gone through all of the cash you had and now you want us to give you more...it is obvious that you don't know how to manage it and in some cases, they are right. This said, please remember they could still have the most amazing idea, product or service and it is just that they haven't had the time for it to succeed because they were closed to understanding how important it would be on the front end to be appropriately financed.

It takes time to develop a business and to develop a customer base. In some cases, this can be a short period of time and in others it can take years. As we said, the difference in business is anything you do impacts both sides of the business equation. In your home you can reduce expenses without generally impacting your income and because of this you are able to pull yourself out the hole created by the unanticipated costs. In business, as soon as you impact expenses there will be an impact in your revenue so there is a fine balance between the two.

Remember in starting a business, you are doing so because you have a dream. You want to be your own boss and to create your own thing and for that you should be commended. In having this dream you will see the world through a set of rose colored glasses and it is only you who can take them off. We will ask our clients what is more important....running a successful business or being right? Learning to run a business is challenging enough in and of itself without putting pressure on you by doing it on an insufficient start-up budget. There is a fine balance between being frugal and being crazy so know going in you need to ask yourself the tough questions like...How long could I exist if there were half the sales I anticipated coming in for a period of six months? What would happen if I couldn't pay myself for six months? What would be the long term impact if I had to get out of a lease?

In terms of your start-up expenses, determine which ones are absolutely critical and which ones are the nice to haves. For example, do you need to have a brand new desk or would a second hand one work? Make sure you are paying for those which are more critical first, and don't commit to buying the less important until absolutely necessary. For example, if you developing a store front operation focus on what your customers will see and don't go and buy the staff room equipment until just before you are going to open. You will absolutely need the display fixtures however you might not need the high end inventory racks for the storage room. Plan well and stay within your budget during start-up, period. From day one you need to build the thinking of how do I do this a different way? You will also need to ask yourself what is important to me in building this business?

LEARN FROM THOSE WHO HAVE GONE BEFORE YOU

Being an entrepreneur or business owner can be one of the most rewarding experiences you will ever have. It can also be one of the most challenging and lonely things you do. All successful business owners we know have a network and group around them to challenge them in their thinking. Sometimes it is a loosely formed group of individuals or sometimes it is a more structured group which acts more as a Board of Directors. They generally are a diverse group of people, who come from varied backgrounds and from various businesses and industries. Whichever way they are structured and the makeup are not important. What is important is they are made up of strong personalities who think individually and who challenge one another on a continual basis.

Look around you. Who are you spending time with? Know five years from now, you will be like them. Nothing could be truer, than this statement. Birds of a feather flock together. If you want to be different from what you are today, find someone who exhibits the traits you want to have and spend time with them. We call this modeling. In order to model, we have to find exceptional mentors.

We have all heard about the importance of mentors. Do you have one? Do you have many? Who do you know who is exceptional at what they do? If you are in business, find a mentor, a coach, someone who can assist you to do what you are working to accomplish. Find someone who has done what you want to do and who is proven, someone who is accomplished. Too often people spend time in their circles with people who want to accomplish something similar to them, but who as of yet, have not done so. It is comfortable being around others like you, but you are trying to create something different now. So find those people not like you in this regard. It is great to work and strive, however the fastest way to accomplish something is to do it as the professional does it.

Take for example Tom Kite, absolutely one of the greatest golfers of his time with nineteen PGA tour victories. Tom was the first on tour to reach $6 million, $7 million, $8 million, and $9 million in career earnings. Now, here is what is interesting with him, he is legally blind, 5' 9" and 170 lbs. Athletically, he is nothing special. His swing was far from impressive on the drive whereas his short game was noted as strong. He was also noted for changing his putting techniques mid tournament due to his suffering from "yips". Based on all of this, what made Tom such an exceptional golfer? Simply put, it started in his mind and he was willing to improve his game by using those available around him to assist him. He was willing to play with the best in order to become the best.

Tom Kite was one of the first professional golfers to use a sports psychologist. Again, this demonstrates his understanding of the mental side of the game. However, he also used coaches like Bob Toski in the 1970s to improve his swing speed by ten miles per hour. Tom also employed one of the greatest golf coaches ever, Harvey Penick. Harvey is a Hall of Fame Coach in the golf world.

It is expected in professional team sports that we use coaches and mentors. Now it has become an integral part of the game even in individual sports. Would you agree it works? We have a term we call, the "coffee creamer syndrome". It is when you see something in one context and yet never think about it in another one. In other words we disregard something which could work because it is in another, seemingly unrelated area. If you believe coaching works in sports then who are you using as a coach or mentor in your business? Have you or can you identify someone who is proven in what they have done? Someone who is much larger and more accomplished than yourself and who is willing to share what they know, and how they got there with you? Remember if you want to be somewhere completely different in five years, you need to find someone excellent at what you want to create. Spend time with mediocrity and that is what you will get. Even if you are excellent at taking their information you will recreate with excellence their mediocrity.

Earlier, we used the term modeling. Modeling is a process we do intuitively and naturally, however, it can also be much more effective when you are conscious of the process and with volition when you put it to work for you. To understand modeling, think of it this way. In general when it comes to physical abilities, people are typically cut from the same mold. If this is the case, then why when we look at professional athletes do some perform at levels far greater than others? Tom Kite is a prime example. He was an average guy of physical stature although he was legally blind, which should have made it near impossible for him to accomplish what he did. What made Tom special was his approach to the game in his thinking and in how he channeled that thinking to produce results. Tom used the greatest coaches and resources around him to hone his thinking and game. He spent 175 weeks as a top 10 ranked golfer in the early 1990's as a result and was inducted into the World Golf Hall of Fame in 2004 based on all of his accomplishments. That is world class and demonstrates someone who understands the importance of using tools and resources around him to constantly improve his game.

As people sometimes, we make it really hard on ourselves. For some of you, you may believe that you need to figure out everything for yourself or it simply won't be your own accomplishment. We believe it is those who figure out how to find short cuts who are the smart ones and who go on to create something different. Really, why make something harder than it needs to be? These traits are habit and they encompass who you are. Our guess, Tom Kite will mirror the aspects of excellence in other areas of life because it is a mindset he employs. It will be a big part of why he is in demand now as a speaker and absolutely in his business endeavors today such as golf course design.

To understand modeling, first understand this. It is your job to learn from your mentor. Traditionally, people believe it is the mentor's job to share what he or she knows about their field of excellence. Here is the crux of the issue if you think this way. Pick anything you are amazing at and ask yourself, "What makes me amazing at this"? Do you even know? Do the things you talk about really have anything to do with it and how do you know? If you were to share what you thought was important would the person you are sharing the information with be able to do what you are telling them to do? To take this even further, how often in the work place do we explain a process to someone only to find they are unable to replicate what you are sharing with them?

In our work we find this is one of the greatest issues in the operation of a business. The way we have learned to transfer information around how to do something is not all that effective. Let's go back to the premise of your mind and how you think. Let's say you are showing someone how to do a particular task. For example say in selling, it requires them to speak with people they do not know. You are perfectly comfortable in doing this and have developed a belief system around your ability to communicate your product or service to people. Now, let's assume the person you are mentoring holds some belief of self that is limiting around their ability to meet and influence someone they have not known for some time frame. Do you believe they can get the same result as you? Your beliefs will have you take different actions and because it is simply a part of you, how would you know you need to tell them this is important in their ability to sell the way you do? They will never be able to produce your results until they change the belief.

In this example, you can explain how to cold call, the process of explaining the product or service and the building of interest in your product till the cows come home. The limiting belief of self will never let this person believe this process will work for them, and they will achieve the results in line with their belief set. On the other hand, if they were to ask you not only about the process but also about what you believe as you cold call, it would have you consider what you do believe when you are performing this task. They would be able to ask you questions which you never would have considered and their own unique filter set would have them identify far different questions than what you would have consider important.

Back to modeling, and in understanding the process of modeling someone. The first thing we believe is it goes beyond the "how" of the physical doing in order to learn to do something with excellent results. Sure "how" is part of it, but only a small part of it. This is why traditional mentor relationships often do not work effectively. To transfer the ability of someone else to you, your filters need to be "tuned in" as theirs are in order to replicate the behavior with any degree of accuracy. Simply put, if you wish to model someone on how they do something you need to take responsibility to understand how they process and filter their world. You need to understand how they interpret their world and the feedback they receive in order to achieve the result. In other words, you need to ask them what they are thinking when they doing what they are doing. If you wait for them to tell you, chances are it is pretty unconscious to them so they won't even think about telling you.

To do this, the following is a list of things which are helpful to understand:

Find someone who is worth modeling, who has done what you wish to achieve;

Find out their beliefs, values, and strategies for doing this particular task;

Find out about their physiology, as they do it; and,

Install all of this in yourself.

To further explain this, say I wanted to increase sales in my business. I would want to find someone who has done this and who does it very well. Once you have this, ask them what they believe about themselves, their environment, others including clients/customers and their product or service. Find out everything they believe around that topic and keep track of it all. Then find out their values around the topic. To understand values think of it this way, values drive us in what we do. They are what motivate us in advance and they are how we feel after we have done it. You can elicit values around this task by asking them, "What is important to you about doing sales?" for example. Ask them several times and make a list of values. For each value, you may even wish to do some further exploring by asking them what the specific value means to them. One of the most common mistakes in this area is the assumption you understand what they are saying. To be clear, chances are you don't. If you want to check out what we mean ask a few people around you what is important to them about respect (respect as a value). You will see people all hold different ideas around this.

Once you have the list of beliefs and values, now you can go into the process of how they do whatever it is you want to learn. Ask them, the sequence of what they do. Find out the complete order and find it out in detail. Finally, ask them how they feel when they do it. Note these feelings, but equally important notice, their physiology, that is, how do they carry themselves, what is their body language. Head up, eye contact, shoulders back, breathing deeply and slowly as an example. Note all of this.

Now in the final step, take all of these things: the beliefs, the values and the physiology and try them on initially without doing anything. Notice how you see the process now versus how you did it previously. Do you think differently about it? If not, take all of the beliefs and values and physiological and build a picture of how that would look in your mind. Focus on the picture in your mind and notice how you feel. This is the state and thinking you need to hold as you do the process you are modeling.

Take all of this and go do it. Now, this is important so read this and follow this every time. Do everything as the expert did until you are as good as they are. Too often, people will decide ahead of time that something is not important and remove it from the process. It may be important, it may not be, but you have never duplicated the result so how would you know? Steps not critical to the duplication of the idea are called idiosyncrasies. You cannot know what is important and what is idiosyncratic until you can duplicate the process equally as well. To determine this, remove one step each time you do it and notice if it impacts your results. Essentially, you are matching your model and filters to a model that works and this is why it works.

Here is the funny thing, people at times will tell us this is too hard or this is not possible. They say, "I believe what I believe, that is what makes me who I am". All we will say is, "Then great, keep doing what you are doing, and maybe you will get the result or maybe you don't really want to. When you do, you will do what you need to do, to do it." We believe mentoring or modeling can work well if the traditional roles are reversed.

For a moment, let's go back to the start of this chapter. Remember we said look around at who are you hanging around with? That is who you are becoming and five years from now, or sooner, this is who you will be. This is true because we model unconsciously all the time. This is how we all learn to do what we do and adapt to our environment. Our filters or our beliefs, values and strategies are constantly being impacted by our environment. You know how to behave in your world today, but think of how you may behave if you were living in an entirely different environment, such as one with war and fighting. Would you begin to behave differently? It is just when you are unconscious to modeling you may tend to take the slow boat. When we work with volition, we do it quickly with repeatable results.

I know you can agree the mental side of professional sports is critical. If you believe this, then believe the exact process is in play in your business. We are like machines in how we think and work and there is good and bad news to this. The good news is you are in charge of your mind therefore your results and the bad news is you are in charge of your mind and therefore your results. What are you doing to get in charge of it? Are you utilizing excellence around you to create excellence? Are you finding those whom perform at high levels in areas you do not and spend time with them? Learn from those who have gone before you and short cut yourself to success.

SUMMARY

We sincerely hope you have gained some insight in to what it means to get into business although we know you will never really know what it means until you do it. Those already having made the transition to business can attest to this fact. Like we said, we love what we do and we love being in business. Some of the material, we have presented might have seem to be to scare you off. Remember you are being tested in your conviction around getting into business. We want to make sure to present the material in the most open and honest way possible. We work with business leaders and entrepreneurs on a daily basis, and these are the same things we hear over and over from these people, when we ask them what it was like for them when they first began.

Each business leader or entrepreneur is different and like we said, there is no "one size fits all" solution when it comes to being successful in business. As we surveyed our friends and clients, we know some of them struggled in some areas and others didn't struggle at all in those same areas. It will be the same for you as you get in business.

Of course we know some of this you may have known or even heard before, however like we said in the beginning, it was meant to test your conviction around being in business. For some of you, you may have decided that maybe now isn't the time. For others, you may have adjusted your plans slightly and intend to enter the game on a different scale. Some of you will have seen some of the challenges with excitement and are already making plans to go. Any which way, we are excited for you and we know you have the ability to succeed if you have the desire and the smarts.

We have compiled what we believe to be the critical components of what you have read, so you can keep them close at hand.

Your thinking and your environmental influences will be massive in relation to your success:

Choose to be at cause. When you are at effect to your environment and to your thinking then you are powerless to change it. When you hold the thinking that somehow you created this situation as a means to learn and grow, you can recognize what you need to learn and go on to create something different:

Anytime you decide you want to do something there will be forces around you which will test your conviction to do it. The more you use these to build your conviction, the more focused you will become in achieving your outcome;

Each of us is surrounded by people who are more than willing to give us advice. Make sure you take the advice of people who have been there and who have done it. Use that advice to test your convictions;

Successful business owners have a network and group around them to challenge them in their thinking. They learn from the best and in doing so, short cut their own learning in order to be able to achieve success quickly;

Notice who you are hanging around and know you will be them in five years. If you want to be excellent at something, then you need to model excellence;

"Learning is not a product of schooling but the lifelong attempt to acquire it" and in the case of the entrepreneur, this is absolutely the truth. It is not about what specifically you know when you start up a business as much as what you are open to learning quickly along the way. That is be curious; and,

There are typically three categories of people. Those who are closed, those who are arrested and those who are open. Entrepreneurs need to always be open to new ideas and opportunities if they hope to grow their business.

For those of you early on in your business always remember:

Time is money. Until you become established as a business and have employees, for every day you are not on your game or which you take away from your business, will impact the revenue of your company. The running of your business will likely fall to those times when your customers are not buying, likely meaning after hours;

If you haven`t anticipated the hidden costs in financing your start up, you will be forced to reduce your expenses which will ultimately impact your ability to generate sales. In a business you are constantly dealing with both sides of the equation;

It is easier to ask for money and receive financing in the beginning rather than when you are in trouble;

In terms of your start-up expenses, determine which ones are absolutely critical and which ones are nice to haves. Make sure you pay for those which are more critical first and don't commit to buying the less important until closer to the time you need them;

When you first get started, running a business is like having two full time jobs. The first one is doing what you do in having a business and the second one is in learning to run a business. It takes time to create the things which will free up time, so you have more time to do those things you want to do; and

In business you have many different bosses and they all come with their own list of demands for you. While you are the boss of your company, remember when you have employees they will want what they want right now in your current situation and they will expect you to provide it.

As you develop and work to grow your business, understand your value:

If you don't know what you are worth, how will anyone else;

You need to figure out and communicate the value you add as a business to your customers and clients;

You differentiate yourself from your competitors through your value proposition;

You can't do everything yourself if you really expect to grow and build your business. You need to be aware when it would be more cost effective to have someone else involved and you need to focus your energy to creating the revenue to cover these costs; and,

You need to know much your product or service is worth and you need to be prepared to own that. If you discount too often, before long your product or service will be worth the price plus the discount all the time.

Each day you operate in business you will be required to make decisions, be ok to make a decision, be okay to make a mistake:

You are going to make mistakes. It is an integral part of how you learn and grow as long as you give yourself a break and keep moving forward. The only time a mistake is a problem is when you let it stop you;

Smart is about the ability for someone to think beyond the circumstances present right here, right now. We believe smart comes down to being able to think beyond the convention of group think;

Something which is a fact today can simply be a fallacy tomorrow so be careful about what you choose to believe;

Understand the rules and yet be willing to push up against convention in order to create something different;

There is no "one size fits all" solution to business. As an entrepreneur you need to continue to expand your flexibility which means you need to continually be pushing yourself. Potential is nothing until it is actualized;

If you are afraid of making a mistake, know never making a decision in and of itself, can also be a mistake;

You will gather as much information as you have time to collect and will never have enough information to proceed until the point you need to make a decision. Make decisions quickly and know you can always change your mind in changing conditions;

People are drawn to certainty. They like to know what they know, to know what they do, and they tend to like to keep things certain. It makes it easier to operate; and

People are incredible problem solvers if they get clear on what they are solving.

In business you have to love what you do:

Be "daft" about what you do...Driven, Attentive, Focus and Thrifty. Find the thing you are crazy about and you will figure out how to be successful doing it. Someone has to be successful so why not you;

If you hate what you do in your own business then the work you do becomes a job. Avoid the shades of grey and love what you do; and

Being attentive to the bigger picture allows you to take advantage of opportunities others will miss. Good business is driven around a return on investment. If what you are doing is not driving a return on investment, then stop doing it.

Your friends and family are important to you and they really do want to see you succeed. In this support remember:

Our friends and family will tell us what we want to hear because they want to be supportive, however if they buy from you, they may believe you should give them a deal and you will feel obliged to give them one;

Consider family and friends buying from you as "gravy" in your business planning. Your business case should be able to stand alone; and,

Thank your friends and family for their support in ways that are meaningful to them and not in ways which lock you in over the long term. At some point, you will have paid back the debt you feel you have and will become "stuck" in a situation which will not be good for any of you. You need to act now as you plan to go forward.

As you see there are a lot of different ideas and concepts we have presented in this book. There are certainly other points which we could have discussed, however we will leave these for the next book.

Unlike the gentleman on the airplane who gave me the advice not to get into business, we will tell you owning your own business is really an amazing experience if you are eager to take on new challenges. There will be moments when it will be hard and there will be moments when you will question whether you did the right thing. We know this because it happened to us. At the same time there will be moments of great success and triumph and with focus and determination before long the amazing side will outweigh the other. As we said in the beginning, you will never gain the type of experience you will get from operating your own business doing anything else. You will never get the self satisfaction or sense of accomplishment you will get from being in complete charge of you.

We know you will have taken some piece of value from this and because of that, please share this message with those around you who may be interested in starting their own business, whatever that maybe. As we said in the beginning, we are committed to the growth of small to medium business as the means of driving our economies. There is success in business. When our economy is strong, it makes for healthy communities, it provides a brighter future for our children, it creates jobs and it allows us to live our dreams. Together we can increase the leverage and status of small business owners to inspire our next generation. You will be making that difference in creating your own company and with each successful company which is created, we move one step.

We wish you much success...create performance by living your dream

**It Is What It Is,
Or Is It....**

Available at <u>www.siere.ca</u> and amazon.ca

It Is What It Is, Or Is It...All About Business bridges the thinking between the traditional business world and the psychology of generating peak performance to provide insight into the thinking that is required today to meet the demands of our fast paced and often uncertain business climate.

Your organization is a reflection of your thinking as a leader, owner or manager. A true understanding of what this statement means and how you can harness the power within holds the key to creating a significant breakthrough in performance for you and your organization. Those individuals who are committed to adapting their own thinking, in this ever changing business environment, create the unique competitive advantage that ultimately drives new levels of performance.

After working with countless business leaders, owners and managers, Jeff and Cathy have found there is a common thread to what sets apart the exceptional from the average. Simply stated, they interpret the world around them differently and in doing so, they not only capitalize on opportunity, they create it. It is in how they think.

What if the convention of business was locking you up from creating more? What if you could generate more abundance, value and wealth simply in becoming aware of how your thinking is impacting your performance? What if you could remove uncertainty and fear, in order to become clearer on what you are driving as a leader, owner or manager? What if?

[i] http://dictionary.reference.com/browse/daft?s=t
[ii] http://www.asktheharvardmba.com/2009/07/03/how-many-graduating-harvard-mbas-start-their-own-businesses/
[iii] http://en.wikipedia.org/wiki/Attention_deficit_hyperactivity_disorder
[iv] The Davinci Method, Garret Loporto

END NOTES